One Word at A Time

Trude Steele Norman

Cock-A-Hoop Publishing, L.L.C.
Tulsa, Oklahoma

One Word at a Time

by Trude Steele Norman
with Roy Caddell

2002 2001 2000 99 98 5 4 3 2 1

Library of Congress Catalog Card Number: 98-072144
ISBN 1-889734-01-2

Published by Cock-A-Hoop Publishing, L.L.C.
P.O. Box 4358
Tulsa, Oklahoma 74159
(918)747-5530

Edited by E. Andra Whitworth, Cock-A-Hoop Publishing
Book design by Karen Kingsley Litchfield, Mad House Graphics
Cover illustrations by Susan L. Smith, Chicago

Printing by Hoffman Printing, Muskogee, Oklahoma

For May, Gloria and Marnell
. . . and my Grandfather

My deepest appreciation goes to Andra Whitworth and Herb Beattie, who took a chance on this manuscript and persevered over long months — and to my husband Mike, who gave up great quantities of my time.

CONTENTS

INTRODUCTION   viii

THE GAUNTLET   X

THE MEETING   1

DAY ONE   *Concrete and Challenges*   7

DAY TWO   *Jump Starting*   13

DAY THREE   *Walt Disney and Inflection*   19

DAY FOUR   *The Printed Word*   27

DAY FIVE   *Magic and Memories*   39

DAY SIX   *Stupid is Not a Label*   48

DAY SEVEN   *Tenacity and Progress*   51

DAY EIGHT   *Hazel and Words*   59

DAY NINE   *Diction on Paper*   67

DAY TEN   *The Rocky Road of Shame*   75

DAY ELEVEN   *Building Blocks*   84

DAY TWELVE   *Trouble and Explanations*   92

DAY THIRTEEN   *New England Friends*   100

DAY FOURTEEN	*The Walls of Jericho*	106
DAY FIFTEEN	*The "Flutterin' Truck"*	113
DAY SIXTEEN	*To, Too and Two*	122
DAY SEVENTEEN	*The Ultimate Scarlet Letter*	130
DAY EIGHTEEN	*Auto Mechanics and Word Mechanics*	139
DAY NINETEEN	*Good News and Bad News*	151
DAY TWENTY	*Hat Bands and Numbers*	160
DAY TWENTY-ONE	*Gibberish and The Real McCoy*	166
DAY TWENTY-TWO	*Roy Caddell's D-Day*	177
REFLECTIONS AND IMPOSSIBLE DREAMS		182
AFTERWORD		185
ROY CADDELL'S BIG WORD LIST		187

INTRODUCTION

Why me? Why not me. . . .? This is a story I could not *not* write. From Day One, I was hooked. The man mesmerized me. When a person starts writing, they better have good cause. I do. Some things you simply don't do for money.

First. I wrote for Roy. His startling revelations and trust struck chords in my soul that would not be quieted. This man standing before me was flesh and blood, he represented one-fifth of the people of my country. Those are alarming statistics that would shake the very foundations of our forefathers.

Roy Caddell was one of many, the Tip of the Iceberg. He knew it and I knew it. But, *he* was the one I could help.

Second. I wrote because I am a journalism major. Writing is my passion and as intrinsic to me as breathing. Black ink runs in my veins. I love the process and the end result.

When I first agreed to become a literacy tutor, I never dreamed I would be writing a book. But, twenty minutes with Roy Caddell and I knew I had been given something special.

His simplistic words overwhelmed me. They kept tugging at my heartstrings and would not let go. His mode of expression was like none I had ever heard, a language and reference all its own. The more he spoke, the more I wrote. This is the result.

Third. I wrote for all the Roys I do not know, and for two dear little boys I did know — Charlie and Donald. Years ago I began grade school with these cousins. They lived at the city dump, in shanties. They wore ragged clothes, but they were my friends. I loved them.

They never would believe I have remembered them these many years, always with fondness and the passionate hope that life has been kind to them. But the ever-present hurt I saw from their eyes has haunted me. I have wondered if my two childhood friends learned to read. Oh, how I hope so — but, I am not sure.

With wisdom beyond her very young years, my mother threw down a gauntlet to me before I began my first grade year:

*"Your smile may be the brightest spot in some child's life, Trude. You
do not know the paths these other children have trod — through no
fault of their own. Remember that, and always, always make them feel
better for having been around you. Take an interest in them. Be their
friend. You might be the only one they have. . . ."*

Why I can recall her words so vividly after nearly fifty years, I do not
know. Such a challenge to an impressionable young mind is not laid quietly to rest. Her simple admonishment and charge became a banner
raised. Her innate insight became my life's rudder. I did not know it
then, but Roy Caddell was penciled into my agenda.

Tucked away somewhere, I still have that first-grade picture, with
me standing in the middle of the front row, a huge smile on my face and
my arms folded in proud defiance — Charlie Byford and Donald
Blakely on either side. I did not care where *I* stood that day. I bloody
well did care where *they* stood!

When I looked closely into Roy Caddell's eyes five long years ago,
instantaneously there was that look that has hounded me. The look I
have seen on a thousand faces, in ten thousand eyes: The look of want,
and of need — and of secrets and pain beyond my imagination.

Perhaps this man was incarnate of my childhood friends. Perhaps
not. Either way, it was simply my turn to reach out and help someone
up, for no reason.

Thus, my bottom-line for writing this book. I hope you enjoy reading it as much as I have enjoyed writing it. Roy and I both "Thank you,"
from the bottom of our hearts. . . .

Trude Steele Norman
Summer 1998

THE GAUNTLET

"Trude, lookin' back, if I didn't know no better, I'd
think this was all a dream. . . ."

He tried turning left legally. He could not read the sign posted above the intersection. Embarrassed and grateful no one honked at him, he sat through three lights before giving up. He turned anyway. I was puzzled when he told me of this and, after class, drove to see his predicament. PROTECTED LEFT TURN ON GREEN glared down from the highway sign. Immediately, I understood. "Left Turn on Green" he could read. The word "Protected" . . . ? No way.

His only response was, "Why cain't they make all a them the same, f'r people like me?" I had no answer.

We with education cannot imagine. Read a road sign, scan a menu, look for a street name, decipher a prescription, find a business locale, read a map, address an envelope, peruse the morning paper over coffee, look at a label for cleaning instructions, fill out a job application — then Stop. Now go back and try to decipher our privileged world and its mundane activities through the warped, narrow lens of illiteracy. Suddenly, the waters look very muddy.

Such was the scenario in which Roy Caddell found himself. He was 64 years old and his one goal in 1994 was to be able to read a newspaper. Five years later, he succeeded beyond his wildest imagination.

He read a lengthy article and missed only forty-four hard words; even those, he tried. He was overjoyed with his attempt, his buttons were popping. I was near tears.

I had watched this man struggle over what I considered common, everyday words for fifty long months. Had I not sat beside him on a battlefield strewn with shame I could not have imagined, his world would have remained forever in my dark ages.

Think about it. We with education read and write as we choose, ferreting out words important in our world. Words are relevant only as they relate to my life and yours. We who are educated do not write solely as we speak. We write what we want, when we want.

The uneducated do not have such luxury. Young and old, they are shackled by their limitations — and scribble whatever they can. They "write" pictures. They "write" jumbled letters that are unrecognizable as words. Frequently, their efforts look like chicken scratches, unreadable gibberish.

These people do not have the same choices we have, it's as simple as that. The lives of the illiterate are limited totally by their inability to read. They live under the slavery of their illiteracy. They did not choose this life for themselves. No one would.

Let's get some definitions clear here. Even though the federal government "no longer uses these terms," they are applicable. Any person who cannot read and write, in legible form, is totally illiterate. A person is functionally illiterate when their reading and writing skills are not above a fifth-grade level.

Under the National Institute for Literacy findings, current federal government guidelines are divided into five groupings: Level 1 being the lowest and Level 5 the highest.

Government statistics report at least one-fifth of the American adult population do not read and write at all. They are in Level 1, the lowest 20 percent of our nearly 260,000,000 population.

Level 2 government findings include another 28 percent of adults who are deemed functionally illiterate. Level 1 and Level 2 figures comprise nearly 50 percent of our adult population.

Government findings further show another 30 percent of the adult populace within our country who read, write and comprehend at the third, or mid-level.

That leaves 20 percent of us who are highly educated and perform at the two top levels of U.S. Government Literacy standards! Shocking.

Let me put it another way. Two, perhaps three, of every five Americans cannot read in its entirety what is printed on this page. They "readt w'th blind spots," as though words are not printed on paper.

Daily, 50 percent of American adults are forced to skip over what they do not know. These nonreaders miss the context of printed matter: Complete comprehension is not an option for them. Guessing is.

There is no mandated law for compulsory education in our federal constitution. Such requirements are left to state governments. States have minimal educational requirements, below which state educational standards cannot fall. The State of Oklahoma Constitutional law, page 161 under "Article 4, Compulsory school attendance," reads as follows:

"The Legislature shall provide for the compulsory attendance at some public or other school, unless other means of education are provided, of all the children in the State who are sound in mind and body, between the ages of eight and sixteen years, for at least three months in each year."

New laws are being implemented in which a "child must know how to read by the third grade." Sounds ideal, utopian. But what about children who drop out before the fifth or sixth grade? Will their reading skills be sufficient? Do we, as a government, go knocking on doors to find each of these children? I think not.

Educational bureaucrats have trouble tracking children who drop out. You cannot become a statistic if you never answer your doorbell to talk to a census taker. Too many of these uneducated people all but evaporate.

Yet, they are out there — affecting our demographics and our cash flow. The U.S. Department of Labor "estimates illiteracy cost taxpayers $5 billion annually in welfare and unemployment alone, and billions more in unrealized tax revenue."

And, "Ninety percent of Fortune 1000 executives expressed concern in a recent survey that low literacy is hurting their productivity and profitability."

Tragically, the face of illiterate America has become a national blight of incalculable measure. The bottom line remains that, often, a person cannot get a job if they cannot read.

Toleration can be a good word or a bad word. To tolerate human differences with compassion for our fellow man is a good thing. To tolerate illiteracy for our nation is a bad thing. It is an unacceptable educational standard.

Our forefathers built this country upon educational and religious freedoms. Freedom in modern society is contingent upon the ability to read and write so others can understand you. Nothing else is acceptable.

We have regressed in a basic tenet of American democracy when millions of adults and children do not know how to read and write proficiently! To tolerate illiteracy as an educational yardstick for our country is a sham, a shell game.

The federal government keeps putting out reams of papered jargon to let us know they are doing their job in educating our populace. I do not question their intentions. I question their results. Statistics can be manipulated to reflect almost anything, positive or negative.

But – when 90 percent of juvenile delinquents do not read above a fifth-grade level; when incarceration is at an all-time high with prisons and jails overflowing with adults who fall into the lowest two reading levels; when welfare rosters are chronically full with adults who have dropped out of school; when employers cannot find literate skilled labor; when errors on job sites result in huge losses as workers cannot read simple instructions; when health care is gravely affected by people who injure themselves because they cannot read labels on medicine; when teen pregnancy statistics are closely linked to low levels of literacy; when traffic courts overflow with students who do poorly in school, particularly in areas of reading and math — we have problems in this country of gargantuan proportions.

Something is drastically wrong when our nation pours billions of dollars into education, and still nearly 50 percent of our people cannot read. The lowest 20 percent of illiteracy statistics was not where Roy Caddell wanted to end up, it was not acceptable to him.

Nowhere is illiteracy acceptable, and certainly not for the most powerful nation on earth. It is degradingly deplorable. We have come to a low point in America when rational, thinking, educated leaders accept mediocrity. Mediocre education as the norm is never acceptable.

The chicanery is that we educated people have bought the programmed rhetoric that the quality of education is going up. In reality, it is not. *Educational standards go up only when illiteracy goes down.*

The problem with literacy is not the amount of time each child spends in school: It is social promotion, or the automatic passing of children to the next grade level, whether or not that child can read or write!

Solutions to the annihilating issue of an illiterate nation are not endless "think tanks." Solutions are "one-on-one" time shares: One who reads gives time to teach one who cannot read, be they adult or child.

The American dream is for all children to stay in school, but for many this is only a pipe dream. In every household, the bottom line is providing for family; often this equates to eating versus learning. Dropping out of school becomes fact in countless homes. The question is not *if*, but *when* will their children drop out . . . ?

Will they drop out to sustain themselves and enter the workforce with competency — or will they drop out to more firmly entrench themselves in a standard of living they do not wish to pass on to their children?

Sadly, too few of these children who drop out ever return. Silently, obscurely, child-adults enter mental sweat shops and quickly become hardened numbers on government demographic charts.

You think you do not know these people. You are wrong. You and I pass people who live in our communities every day who cannot read. Often we do not recognize them because they look exactly like us: Average American Citizens, Joe Blow Next Door.

I would have passed Roy Caddell a dozen times over and never once realized his sullen countenance was the product of his shame of illiteracy. The fault was mine, not his.

Let me throw out a major stumbling block for those seeking help learning to read. You who have the gift of adequate reading skills, try finding the national literacy 800 number in your telephone book. I want to wish you good luck. Then try finding a state literacy 800 number to call.

Next try finding your local literacy telephone number, in either the white or yellow pages of your phone book — or, under "public library." Again, good luck.

In large cities, such are listed under "Reading Instruction" in the yellow pages, and under a city public library in the white pages — if there is a separate entry at all under the library heading.

In smaller towns across our county, it is common to find no literacy listing at all. No literacy listing means no help for those who cannot read.

These telephone numbers must be prominently placed in the front of every telephone directory across America. Why is such vital information not listed with the police and fire department numbers, and why is it not listed freely as a public service? Status quo with regards to illiteracy is a cop-out.

While teaching Roy at our local library, I tried in vain for four years to have the literacy telephone number listed on our public library's recording — and anywhere else in the phone book, even offering to pay for such. I could not get past first base.

Only after I became a member of the library board and continued to hound the powers that be, did I make inroads. Five years down the road, our Muskogee Literacy telephone number is given first on the recording when anyone calls the library — and, it will be listed in both the white and the yellow pages, under "Reading" and "Literacy," when the next telephone directory comes out.

That is major progress, but it is reprehensible that I had to vehemently fight such a battle for a public service from a public facility, that affects 50 percent of our populace!

Government officials, educators and others in power to affect such changes within a community should insist on easy public accessibility to reading services. Anything less is unacceptable.

Nonreaders cannot find such services themselves. One missed attempt and too often they give up — and the vicious cycle repeats. Like it or not, the problem of illiteracy will not go away. Quite the reverse, it reproduces itself with alarming regularity.

If you think one literacy tutor or school volunteer cannot make a difference in the life of an adult nonreader, ask my Friend. But be prepared to listen, he is not shy about telling you his reasons for staying in school.

"I wanna be able'ta talk the talk 'n walk the walk like them ed-ucat'dt people do. I wanna be a regular guy. Them highly ed-ucat'dt folks cain't never know how lucky they are 'til they've walk'dt in our shoes. There ain't nuthin' goodt 'bout bein' illiterate.

"When y'ur tot'lly illiterate like I was, y'ur not readty f'r nuthin' when it comes'ta readin' 'n writin'! I was readty'ta learn, but if you ain't got somebody 'ta tell ya and show ya how, you still get it wrong. Someday I hope I won't al-ways hav'ta go hippity-hop along, one wordt at a time — but f'r now, I do.

"This knowledge 'n learnin' has become a passion w'th me. It's like havin' somethin' of value, 'n packin' it w'th me all the time: *I get the* benefit. Bear in mindt here, Trude, I don't wanna be a scholar — jist a plain ole ed-ucat'dt guy. *By the way, what is a scholar, anyways . . . ?*"

Now you know why I have written this book: To give back to this one man something he never could have imagined for himself, not in his wildest dreams.

This manuscript, covering the first workbook in the Laubach series, unfolds the fascinating story of one man's mind as he comes face to face with a literate environment. Within these pages are a glimpse into an obscure world we with education cannot fathom.

With graphic clarity, Roy Caddell's words shouted at me as I began teaching him to read. I do not know which was greater those five years ago: His shock at my world or my shock at his.

He is not unique. He is not alone. He is the hidden face of America, in black and white reality. We need to acknowledge his deadening story.

The national literacy tollfree 800 telephone number is 1-800-228-8813. Oklahoma's tollfree literacy hotline number is 1-800-405-0355.

Aa Bb Cc Dd Ee Ff Gg
Kk Ll Mm Mm Nn Oo P
Ss Tt Uu Vv Ww X
Aa Bb Cc Dd Ee Ff
Kk Ll Mm
Ss Tt Uu Vv Ww
ABCDEFGHI
PQRSTUVW
ABCDEFGHIJ
PQRSTUVWXYZ
QRSTUVWXYZ
ABCDEFGHIJK
PQRSTUVWXYZ
ABCDEFGHIJ
OPQRSTUVW

One Word at A Time

Aa Bb Cc Dd Ee Ff Gg

Kk Ll Mm Nn Oo Pp

Ss Tt Uu Vv Ww Xx

Aa Bb Cc Dd Ee Ff Gg

Kk Ll Mm Nn Oo Pp

Ss Tt Uu Vv Ww Xx

ABCDEFGHIJKL
PQRSTUVWXYZ

ABCDEFGHIJKL
PQRSTUVWXYZ
QRSTUVWXYZ

ABCDEFGHIJK
PQRSTUVWXYZ

THE MEETING

He could be Anyone. Anywhere. You pass him on the street every day and do not know his Shame. Neither did I.

His whole body stiffened at the sound of my horn. Did he honestly think I would not come? We had talked but briefly when I had called, our conversation light. This man was obviously uneasy.

"You'll know me," I finally told him, "because I'm kind of tall and I'll have on a big smile."

"You'll knowt me," he chuckled in response, "'cause I'm kinder short 'n I'll haf me on a *white* cowboy hat."

Turns out we were the same height.

No one on the street that day would have noticed the bright red sports car turning into the back lot. Nor would they have paid heed to the man in the white hat pacing back and forth, if they'd seen him at all. People would have thought he was just there. No big deal. They were too busy with their own hectic lives to pay mind to such trivia. They had places to go and people to see. Such is simply the way of the world these days. Everyone is frantic.

But, if any had bothered to look closely as the lady stepped from her car and the man waited politely, it would have been obvious that here was a meeting of strangers, from vastly different worlds. Why were these two drawn together so early? And what could they ever have had to talk about?

People-watchers would have had a field day with this scenario. Their antennae would have gone up. Bells and buzzers would have started clanging.

The man in the back library lot that morning was skittish, downright jumpy. His pacing took him but a few feet from his warm brown pick-up. He wanted to be able to make a quick getaway if needed, which seemed more than a strong probability. His was a closed face with eyes that registered pain, eyes that made others want to look away — but, they would never have had the chance. His eyes would have left any face long before they saw life. He saw only bodies. He did not want to see anyone. He wanted to be left alone.

He did not smile. That would have been rare. He would not have spoken, unless cornered; and then, his contact would have been as remote as possible: brief, cold, distant, with no hope of closing the gap.

From his compact body it was obvious he had known hard work. There was nothing to spare, either on his frame or in his attitude. He was not a man to push. He would push back, possibly in a most unwelcome way. He would not go out of his way to hurt you. But, he would not go out of his way to help you either.

Somehow, his whole being seemed furtive, as though life were Chinese torture: To be endured, never once enjoyed. His countenance and demeanor were like a wounded animal, whose chief instinct is survival, escape, to get out of harm's way before it is maimed. Again.

Why he came this particular May day, he was never quite sure. In years to come, he could not have given a specific answer. It was totally out of character.

Driving into town that early morning, he had grabbed the wheel of his favorite battered truck and held on for dear life, chain smoking as always. He could not remember finishing one and lighting another. His eyes were on the road, but his mind was ten thousand miles away.

Goodt gosh, man. What is ya doin' drivin' in here when you knowt y'ur wastin' y'ur time? You done triedt this befor'. How many times has ya gots'ta be knock'dt up the side't a the headt 'ta knowt this won't do ya no goodt? Why did ya come? Why din't ya jist tell that lady ya couldtn't make it today? Ya couldta come up with some 'x-cuse. Y'ur goodt at that.

What was the matter w'th ya anyways 'ta wanna go 'n mess up a per-fectly goodt day w'th this here? Hon-estly, Roy Caddell, I done thought you was smarter than that. But, maybe not. This here don't look too bright on anybody's Smart List. But h'it be right up there at the top a the Dumb List.

Ya knowt y'ur hay needs cuttin', 'n fence needs mendin'. How'r them cows gonna feedt 'n water themselves? Ya think somebod' else't is gonna come 'n carry it outta them? Ya must be crazy! They'll still

*be standin' there bellowin' at ya when you's gets home. Ya shore
coulda used't this here gas in that there tractor this afternoon while
y'ur workin'. It was dumb 'ta come here, dumb I tell ya!*

*I'dt turn this ole boy 'roundt if'ns I hadn't toldt her I'dt be there.
Now why'dt I go 'n do that? I shoulda left mysself 'n out. I coulda
toldt her that maybe I'dt be there. That way I coulda chang'dt my
mindt. But I won't never go back on my wordt after I done give it, so's
I mess'dt up there. What was I a thinkin'?*

*Now, man, ya jist holdt on right there. Ya been wantin'ta do this
all y'ur life. That lady soundt'd real nice on the phone, but I'll bet that
was jis'ta git me here. I'll see. Aren't nobody never as nice't as they
want ya 'ta think they are. Hmph. I done gone 'n wast'dt a whole day!*

Fortunately, as he pulled into the back lot, the place was deserted. That
way he could be alone with his cigarettes and his thoughts, and his
watch. He must have looked at that dern timepiece every three minutes,
and at every car that even came close to moving in beside his.

He watched several of the library employees pull up. He knew that's
who they had to be because they all went in the same back door, like
they knew what they were doing there. It was a bloody cinch he had no
idea what he was doing there, "'cept stickin' out like some ole sore
thumb."

*What are ya gonna say'ta her when she comes up? I suppos' y'ur jist
gonna rush right up 'n say, "Hey, Lady. I needt help." She al-readty
knows that, Roy. Why else't do ya think she's comin' f'r? 'N f'r free!
She has'ta haf somethin' else 'ta do.*

*What are ya gonna talk'ta her 'bout? Ya knowt ya don't like talk-
in'ta no-body! But, ya jist cain't standt there like some block a dead
woodt. Ya shore better come up with somethin' real quicklike, 'cause
she saidt she'd be here at straight up nine o'clock, 'n it's near 'ta that
now. Think fast, man. You's gotta talk'ta her. Else't, how is she gonna
knowt how'ta help ya?*

The woman bounding from her car that day was in her early fifties. She
appeared exuberant, friendly. There was a sense of subtle confidence to
her movements that gave credence to the fact that she would tackle the
world for a cause, an underdog. She had before. She would again.

Dressed in jeans, she was tall and slender, with shortish gray-blonde hair. The first characteristics to catch anyone's attention were her direct eyes and radiant smile, which seemed to reach right out and grab you. She was a noticeable presence.

But, hers was a strong personality that seldom minced words. She got right to the point with as much diplomacy and tact as she could muster, which sometimes wasn't enough. Yet, hers was a big heart, she was a soft touch — with quiet steel underneath.

Somehow, her self-assured manner made her seem capable of much. The question was, was she capable of this? He did not know. Neither did she.

In years to come, the man from the brown pickup would call her a "tenacious mentor. Yer tough 'n ruggedt now, Trude. A coach 'n a teacher all in one. One a them cheerleader types. On my side't."

But, originally, he never would have picked her out in a crowd as a remote possibility. He never could have imagined this one woman might become his dearest friend. It was out of the question.

Heading into town that glorious spring morn, her body felt as though it had been through her grandmother's wringer washing machine. Flat. She could not remember feeling such agitation in a very long time.

What in the blazes have you let yourself in for, Trude? You have ten zillion things that need doing, and now you're taking on this. You must be crazy.

This is not a casual thing you are starting here, Friend. This man might know absolutely nothing, and then where will you be? Is the rest of your life going to come to a dead halt while you teach someone to read? Get serious, Lady.

Is your home going to suddenly run itself? Is all that furniture on the back patio going to strip itself? What about friends you told you would help with their decorating? You cannot keep them waiting, that is plain rude. How are you going to fit in finding fabric samples you promised, along with church choir bus driving? Go ahead — figure it out.

You promised yourself you would not take on one more thing for awhile. So why did you agree to do this? Honestly, Trude Norman. Sometimes, either your timing is dern poor or you need your head examined! Sometimes, it's both.

But . . . that poor man sounded scared to death on the phone, like he couldn't wait to get off. He obviously needs help. Big time. Surely, you can fit in another few hours a week to help someone else.

You are always telling people "public service is the rent you pay for the space you occupy on earth." Either pay up, or quit gritching.

The fact of the matter was that she was so excited that morning that she could hardly sit still. This was going to be fun, she could feel it in her bones. She never had done this before, but that did not bother her. There is a first time for everything. This was hers.

She was prepared, of that she had no doubts. She had spent hours getting ready for this day. In literacy classes, it was stressed that initially a tutor must spend time visiting with a student — determining his or her goals, and discovering what had brought them to this point. The "talking part" would be a snap.

Her only point of anxious contention was the actual *teaching* part. The rest she could wing. But on that first day, it was the starting up part that made her stomach feel like the butterflies had already landed for their annual winter hibernation in Mexico.

Immediately as she rounded the library corner, she spotted that white hat glistening in the morning sun, planted atop an older man wearing cowboy boots. Both jumped at her from his stark figure silhouetted against bare pavement. Good gosh, how long had he been there anyway? And why did she think he would be taller?

Her immediate reaction was, "Forget the record books. *This one man cannot read!*" Those dull ledger books always so simplistically state: "One in five Americans cannot read," as if it's no big deal. Those thick books deal in black and white, not technicolor. Welcome to the real world, Lady. This "Number Five" has a name. He is not one of "The Privileged Four." And, this *is* a Big Deal.

Resignation gripped his weathered face as he sharply turned at the sound of her horn, quickly throwing his cigarette as if she might reprimand him later. She distinctly remembered a limp wave and a sick smile as he headed her way. His demeanor told the whole story. The jig was up.

She could not imagine his thoughts at that moment. Someday she would ask him, but not now. Months later, he was to convince her that he "was the one ha'f-scair'dta death." That day, it was a toss-up.

"Hi!" she called, jumping from her car and extending her hand. "I'm Trude Norman and I'm so happy you've come. Thank you."

"And I'm Roy Caddell," he said deferentially, meeting the grasp. "Y'ur happy I've come? You got this all back'ards now. I shouldt be the one's thankin' you f'r takin' y'ur time 'ta come down here 'n help me. I shore do hope this all works out. . . ."

In point of fact, the jig was up on both sides of the fence. How we made it inside the Public Library that first morning, I still cannot remember.

All I recall of my first sighting of Roy Caddell was his incessant pacing — back and forth, up and down, back and forth. Like a robot on a pogo stick, with a white crown and wings, for fleeing.

CONCRETE AND CHALLENGES

*"The best psychology you can use on anyone is to
teach them why they are doing something."*

— *Sister Elizabeth Kenny*

*"Places like this don't ad-vertise much, 'n that's badt.
People like me don't never wanna go ask'dt the smart
people where ya gotta go'ta learn'ta read 'n write. We
don't wanna look dumber than we al-readty are."*

We visited easily for a good hour before getting down to brass tacks, Lesson One in *Book One of the Laubach Way to Reading*. Instantly, I realized Roy did not have his own student text! I wanted to run. I stayed and said nothing. We used my book.

That first day we covered six words: BIRD, CUP, DISH, FISH, GIRL and HAND. We went over each word, studying the beginning letters: the shape and sounds of every letter. I said everything first, with Roy repeating after me — exactly as I had been trained in tutor orientation classes.

We always read from left to right, and always in the proper sequential order. We did not skip around. We went *down* a word chart for that day's lesson, reading and saying out loud each beginning letter of the six words assigned to us for the day. Then we went back *up* that same word chart, forming our mouths carefully to make correct sounds of beginning letters. Next, we went back *down* the same word chart again, repeating the name of each letter, for familiarity and emphasis. Three times we attacked each new letter.

In essence, I would teach this man to read letter by letter, sound by sound, word by word . . . sentence by sentence. It seemed like a good logical progression to me.

For the next nine weeks, we followed this format strictly, week in and week out — changing only the alphabetic letters we studied as they were presented in our lesson manuals. This repetitive structure is vital for all beginning readers. Sameness becomes their security blanket.

We did not deviate in approach so that Roy Caddell would know what to expect each lesson, as well as what I expected from him. In time, this pattern helped him to relax and build needed self-confidence. I liked it. He loved it. He was warming up to our task.

A short story with simplistic pictures accompanied every lesson plan. The story incorporated the same six words we learned with each day's lesson. First, we learned the six new words. Then, we read the story. Once again, consistency. Sameness.

When we began to read that first story, Roy suddenly let me know, "I thank I can readt sum'a them wordts." Sure enough, he could — and, he did. Haltingly, tentatively, in a cadence I would have believed could come only from a first grader.

But, I had no intentions of letting him *think* he was at a first-grade level. It was a tricky position that followed us throughout our early years of learning.

Then and there, I realized I would have to test my faculties to find innovative ways of teaching this man to read. He was bright. I did not want him becoming bored before we ever got started, which quickly could kill us.

Yes, Roy Caddell *could* read some things, but nothing with confidence, nothing with expression in his voice. Absolutely everything he read back to me in those early lessons was verbalized in a dull, flat monotone. Staccato fashion. There was simply no inflection in his voice.

This was a characteristic of illiteracy I had learned in tutor training classes. This outward verbalization is always a dead giveaway for non-readers. I made a mental note to mention these factors to him at a later date. In the meantime, first things first.

"OK, Roy. We are going to tackle these first few lessons slowly, so things will begin to fall into place for you in a logical order. We are going to approach this as if we are building a pyramid. The most important part is the bottom layer.

"You must have a solid foundation on which to build all that is to follow. I do not know exactly where you are needing help in this Education Business, nor do you. That is why you are here. That is why

I have come. I do not want to backtrack, I will not rush you. But, I *will* nudge you." I was looking him dead in the eye without a trace of a smile. He nodded compliance and seemed eager to move on.

So far, so good. He was still breathing, as was I. Soon, we finished that critical first lesson with both of us intact, no small feat. Perhaps now he was grateful he had come, and survived. I did not know. I did not ask. I only know he seemed eager to return.

That first day, I sent Roy home with individual word cards for the six lesson words he had so aptly learned. Such cards had been suggested in tutor training workshops. I followed through. Each new word was printed on heavy cardboard with magic markers. In time, each became his friend. Every lesson we ever had throughout that first workbook involved word cards. How he loved them, fortunately. Eventually, he would have hundreds!

Roy Caddell was surprisingly open to conversation that first morning, though he asked no questions of me. As I listened to the painful outpourings of a man who had lived his adult life in the darkness of illiteracy, I was astounded. Never could I have imagined such degradation.

Little did he know how his descriptive words grabbed like a claw, tearing at my heart, my mind, my being. I could scarcely breathe for fear of missing a word or phrase that would effectively communicate to me his background, his feelings, his world. He seldom looked my way as he talked, as if I were not in the room. Perhaps, it was easier that way.

"When you cain't readt '*n it bothers you*," he slowly began, "you don't want no-body 'ta get close 'ta you. Like, I wouldt *not* let my wife call 'ta

"AFTER TALKIN' TA YA, MAYBE I SEEN A LITTLE GLIMMER A HOPE 'BOUT 'XPOSIN' MYSELF. I SAW A CHANCE IN YOU, EVEN IF IT ONLY LAST'DT TWO WEEKS, I'DT BE THAT MUCH AHEADT. I HADT NUTHIN' 'TA LOSE. IN MY CASE, SOMETHIN' WAS BETTER THAN NUTHIN'."

see if somebod' in our town couldt teach me 'ta readt. I saidt *no ways!* I wouldn't haf none a that!

"So's I made't her look somewheres else't. We al-most give up now, 'cause it took her awhile 'ta find this here place. They don't at-vertize much. 'N that's badt, 'cause people like me don't never wanna go ask'dt the smart people where ya gotta go'ta learn'ta read 'n write. We don't wanna look dumber than we al-readty are.

"The thing 'bout it is, Trude, some people don't care if somebod' else't out there knows they cain't readt. But me? I care! I don't want no-body 'ta knowt I cain't readt! That is strict-ly *my* business.

"Somebod' like me is al-ways on guardt. Ya don't never wanna be put in a position where no-body can call on ya if y'ur out somewheres. Like at church, 'r a sale.

"So's, ya make a joke 'bout everythin' so's ya can al-ways keep ever'body way out here. . . ." He held his arm straight out from his body so I would get the picture. I'd already gotten it.

The Wall. Some people spend entire lives behind that barrier, constantly focusing time and energies to build imaginary fortresses ever higher, ever thicker — to insulate themselves from hurt, from reality, from life.

And the joking to which he alluded? Humor can be a negative as well as a positive. Why can't people just say, "Help"?

Roy Caddell's eyes were sad as he talked. His words were slow in coming to the surface, possibly from fear of judgment by me, possibly from fear of betrayal by a stranger. I could not blame him.

Regardless, the man was in torment, having lived a life of self-imposed isolation. This rapidly became obvious.

He had been serving this life sentence long enough.

"Y'UR PERSONALITY MADE'T A DIFF'RENCE. I DIN'T KNOWT YA ALL THAT WELL, 'N I SHOULDN'T A TRUST'DT YA RIGHT OFF. BUT WHEN YA TOLDT ME THAT IF I EVER SAW YA OUT SOMEWHERES, YA WOULDN'T TELL NOBODY HOW YA KNEW ME . . . THAT WAS REAL CRITICAL 'TA ME."

My job would be to open the windows and doors leading to his mind. My job would be to unshackle him by any means I could. Now I knew why the literacy coordinator had sent this man my way. *This* was definitely going to be a challenge.

Years later, as I referred to this day in our conversations, he would tell me: "Why, ya don't knowt the haf'a it, Trude. Them's jist'a few a the things I coulda toldt ya back then. . . ."

He secretly smiled to himself and looked ahead, peering into worlds I could never fathom.

Secrets and Fear. In tutor training classes we had learned of both. But, hearing words and seeing feelings emanate from another human being are two vastly different creatures. Roy Caddell made faraway statistics stomp into existence to be heard, to be felt.

His world was hardened pain, walking concrete — that set up too quickly in the pit of my stomach, and must have been unbearably heavy for him to carry.

This man was going to be a study in humankind, a lesson in humanity I had never learned. It was about time.

Instinctively, I knew the two of us were about to embark upon the ride of a lifetime, an experience that only comes along once — if you are lucky. I am lucky beyond belief. I call it blessed by God. This quiet, sturdy man was about to embrace my life in ways I could not then imagine on that shiny fourth day of May, 1994.

Why did I so readily take this one man's cause to heart? For one reason only: *He seemed vulnerable.* Look it up in your closest dictionary. Mine says, "capable of being wounded." For another human being to be open to such intense daily suffering grieved me.

"ONE A THE THINGS THAT'S HELP'DT ME THE MOST, 'N ONE A THE THINGS THAT WOULDA MADE'T ME QUIT THE FASTEST, WAS NOT BEIN' PRIVATE. WE HAF 'TA GIVE THIS LIBRARY ALOTTA CREDIT. THESE PEOPLE TREAT'DT US REAL GOODT. THAT'S IMPORT'NT 'TA SOMEONE LIKE ME. ONE WRONG WORDT 'N I MIGHT NOT A BEEN BACK."

I flew home that first day in shock and total exhilaration, still so excited about the prospect of what lay ahead. Yet, my own shallow naiveté left me hurting for someone I barely knew; and ashamed of my narrow, privileged, educated life. These three hours had brought me up short.

Roy Caddell was not the only one deficient in our classroom.

In literacy training classes, I had been told that the library had a large conference room that could be reserved for private tutoring. The room was off to itself, sequestered. The absolute seclusion of that room was pivotal to all Roy Caddell and I ever accomplished.

That solitary space became our own private haven for those few short hours each time we met. There, we could be in our own little world, laughing out loud and verbally punctuating the air with our constant repetition of the innards of the English language.

Because of the sanctity of that room, my friend never felt uncomfortable coming to the library and learning to read. Initially, he did not like that the library staff knew why we were there. Ultimately, he accepted this. The outside world knowing, he could not.

For those first formative months, our privacy was as vital to this man as the oxygen he breathed. He would have quickly withered and died under public scrutiny.

On the days the room was unavailable for use, Roy Caddell preferred not to meet. Period. His primary need was always to be alone, undisturbed, totally isolated.

However, there were times when we arrived at the library and there were scheduling conflicts. It was, after all, a public facility. On such days, stark panic immediately appeared on his face. He wanted to evaporate. Fortunately, we found a compromise and headed outside to the staff picnic table in the warm healing sunshine. It was not a bad trade-off.

Public libraries across America should have such a private sanctuary for literacy tutoring. No matter how small. No matter how dingy. Absolute privacy is the first requirement for adult beginning readers. They must be handled with kid gloves.

That is . . . if you want them to succeed. If you want them back.

DAY
2

JUMP STARTING

"A literate person is not only an illiterate person who has learned to read and write, he is another person. A different person. To promote literacy is to change a man's conscience by changing his relation to his environment."

— *Frank C. Laubauch*

"Roy," I promptly offered the second day, "I owe you an apology. I made our first lesson hard because I did not bring the right student workbook for you. I flat goofed up, and I'm sorry!"

"Well, now, I shore couldn't tell it none. I thought you done jist fine. In fact," he said brightening with a smile, "I wanna keep it up 'cause I knowt I learnt somethin' 'n I feel real goodt 'bout it. I was lookin' forward'ta comin' back here today." His words were rushing out like the spring wind. It felt good.

He had never noticed my error. Getting the right text was an easily remedied oversight, not the end of the world. What was important that first day was that we start out on a positive note. Looks like we did.

Casually, I asked Roy Caddell what his wife thought of his first lesson. Little did I know what my modest question would evoke.

"Well," he slowly began, "she's all f'r it 'n can al-readty tell I learnt me somethin'. But me 'n her

"THERE'S HARDSHIP ON FAMILY WHEN YA CAIN'T DO Y'UR PART, LIKE READIN' 'N WRITIN'. MAYBE IT WAS SELFISH A ME 'TA WANNA COME UP HERE 'TA TRY LEARNIN' THIS, BUT IT HAS A TRICKLE DOWN EFFECT F'R MY FAMILY THAT'S BEEN GOODT. IT'S BEEN GOODT F'R ME, 'SPE-CIALLY SINCE I DONE HAD ME TWO 'R THREE A THEM ADJUSTMENT ATTITUDES."

got in 'ta it this mornin' when she tried'ta get them cards you give me, 'ta haf me say 'em to her befor' she left f'r work. I toldt her that 'No, them's mine, and 'ta leave 'em alone.' I think I kinder hurt her feeling's 'n I'm feelin' pret-ty badt 'bout it. . . ." He was looking at his folded hands resting on the table. He never turned my way.

This was an area of potential conflict I had not considered. Although in training workshops it was mentioned that when one member of a family begins to learn to read, it laterally impacts every other family member. I had not applied such words to this man. My fault.

"Roy," I quietly began when we were safely ensconced in the second-floor conference room, "I should have discussed this with you before you left for home last time. It simply never crossed my mind, and I'm dreadfully sorry."

"T'ain't y'ur fault. It's mine. I shouldn't haf done it."

"Well, let's look at this another way. Your wife has always been there for you, always helped you. Naturally, she wants to help you in this, too. She can be a huge help to you, and to me.

"She can reinforce not only what you are going to learn so quickly, but she can build your confidence level from 'I think I can' to 'I know I can.' I asked if he had ever heard the children's story *The Little Engine that Could?* He had, and quickly grasped my point.

"I guess't I need'ta go home 'n a-pologize 'ta her," he finally offered. "'Cause she was all teary-eyed this mornin' when she left f'r work, but she didn't say nuthin'. She jist left."

How right Frank C. Laubach, the original founder and author of Laubach workbooks was when he wisely wrote, "A literate person is not only an illiterate person who has learned to read and write, he is another person. A different person. To promote literacy is to change a man's conscience by changing his relation to his environment."

Did I ever have a lot to learn! Change. The very word spoke volumes. Without receptiveness within ourselves to new ideas, through a constant willingness to scrutinize our own thought patterns and actions, we are all doomed. Alive, yet dead. Too many of us are locked up tight. Skin is stretched taut over minds as well as bodies. Nothing gets in, or out.

Change to me is a positive. This man had already changed before my eyes and, obviously, before his wife's. Would forthcoming efforts be worth the ride we were embarking upon? I surely hoped so. There were bound to be rough days ahead for Roy Caddell.

Next, we solemnly turned our focus to Day Two's lesson. In addition to the workbook plan for that day, I had brought the first ten words from the list of "300 Most Frequently Used Words," supplied for us in my Tutor Workshop Handbook.

The words included were THE, OF, AND, A, TO, IN, IS, YOU, THAT and IT, which we used in tandem with the lesson words. First we verbally went over these relatively simple "Must Know" words. He did not miss a one, which tickled him. Whether or not he would know them every time in the future, only time would tell.

Next, we quickly perused the previous lesson, which was certainly easier for Roy using his own student workbook. I guess. Poor fellow, you would think your own teacher could start you out with the right book!

Day Two's six new words from our tandem workbooks were LEG, MAN, NECK, PAN, JUMPING and KICKING.

We went over this group in the same exact manner as we had the first. He had trouble with the pronunciation of LEG. He tended to say "Lag" which, I told him, was also a word. But for now, we had to get LEG right. Fortunately, MAN, NECK and PAN gave him absolutely no trouble.

We then turned to JUMPING and KICKING, which were obviously different. I went over the -ING letter combinations of the two words, explaining "these are called Endings. We can add -ING to literally thousands of words and slightly change the way in which a word is used, or its meaning." Roy was listening intently.

"Well, I'll be. I never thought 'bout that bein' a wordt I might knowt, w'th jist that there on the endt," he offered, looking inconceivably first to JUMPING and then to KICKING — and back again.

"These are the things I want you to start looking for, Roy: Words you already may know, that are hidden inside of bigger words you may not know. I do not think you are giving yourself enought credit for what you do know, just because that -ING is tacked onto the end of a word."

With that, I placed my hand over -ING in JUMPING and KICKING and asked him to "read these words to me." This he could easily do. He well understood the concept.

He had no trouble reading both words without their endings. *But he had stood no chance of reading both words as they had been given in our text.*

"Makes sense't," he said brightly, "but I'da never thought 'bout doin' that 'ta try 'n figger out a wordt. I'da jist skipp'dt over it befor' today 'n gone on. I been tryin'ta make this extra hardt on myself. I gots'ta start looking' f'r them wordts I knowt." He was rubbing his chin in amazement that he could grasp even a small part of this "learning to read business."

Roy was thrilled to learn about word endings. When later I pointed out that the letters -ED and -LY can also be added to thousands of words, he quickly interjected, "'N those wouldt be called endin's, too?"

The man was smart. He paid attention. He would learn to read. My job was to stay ahead of him.

Looking for words tucked inside words was not in my teacher manuals. It was my own approach, it simply seemed logical. I would not let even one small learning opportunity pass us by. Each one slowed us down immeasurably. Within reason, that did not matter. My obligation was to teach this man to read, however long it took. How I got there was largely my own choice.

Hundreds and hundreds of times in the months that followed, I would place my hands over parts of words so he could more readily spot *even one tiny word* he knew. I call this Words Within Words.

Thus, we hunted for words inside words every chance we got. Not a day went by that we did not find dozens. As the weeks passed into months, I often would say to Roy, "I cannot not show you this. It's another one of those logical progressions." He knew my meaning implicitly. But, it clicked in his mind another way.

"Oh, yeah, I heard'ta that. I knowt what ya mean. It's like, if I was workin' on some ole car 'r truck. If I tore the engine apart 'n then warn't packin' my toolbox right then, it wouldn't do me no goodt. You gots'ta have ever'thin' all at once'dt befor' you start up. I understandt what you mean."

The only nuance was that Roy pronounced our new attack plan as "log-icle pro-sessions." Quite honestly, I liked his pronunciation better. This simple approach of Words Within Words would become, for us, a standard method of operation throughout long years of learning.

If Roy could recognize any part of our English language, then immediately we would be ahead. It was becoming increasingly obvious to me that he needed every advantage I could offer.

How I hoped these radical measures and deviations from Laubach's outlined teaching method would prove worthwhile and accurate; and not confuse my friend. I would have to take my chances. I play life for the long run, no matter how long it takes. *This* was going to take a very long time.

Let me clarify something here. None of this complex reading business came easily for this man. Initially, he did not even know to begin his writing at the left hand side of the paper. He agonized over the most minute detail of the educational process. He struggled daily.

Originally, every concept we tackled was effort. Each word was a chore to pronounce. Roy Caddell had no confidence in his own abilities, and only a rudimentary knowledge of reading skills. He did not know enough about words to know where he needed help, where he was deficient. He only knew he was.

Every day was a totally new ball game, with more rules and added variations to the very rules he

"I HAD ME A DESIRE SINCE I WAS 19 'R 20 'TA DO SOMETHIN' 'BOUT MY ED-UCASHUN. COMIN' UP HERE BROUGHT SUM 'A MY HOPES TO THE SURFACE, MAYBE I SAW IT WAS MY LAST CHANCE. SOMETIMES, THERE'S ONLY ONE TRAIN OUT 'N YA BETTER CATCH IT, 'SPECIALLY IF YOU'VE MISS'DT THE LAST THREE 'R FOUR."

had just learned. Every day he was fearful he would strike out — or be ejected from this new game.

He brought only strong desire to the table, and a joyful willingness not often found in people of any age. Every tutor wishes for such a student. These men and women, old and young, are the future gold medal winners in Literary Olympics.

Why had this man reached for help now? I was not sure. Nor did I ask. Why a grown man of sixty-four would intentionally put himself to such endurance tests was beyond me. All he offered was, "I jist wants 'ta learn't if I *can 'r I cain't* learn'ta readt." His obvious bottom line.

How steadfast he would be, I did not know then. No tutor can ascertain that. Only time provides such answers. Either pupils show up for the next lesson, or they do not. No one can make them come. They have to want it.

It appeared this one man wanted this, badly. By now, I was betting that Roy Caddell would be back every single time. Too bad I did not lay big money on the wager.

WALT DISNEY AND INFLECTION

Roy Caddell had never read a story, not even to himself. And certainly, he had "never readt anythin' out loudt befor' comin' down here."

Walking upstairs the third day, Roy casually leaned over to whisper, "Ahh. See that man over there? I think he's jist like me 'n he cain't readt ne'ther. I'm pretty smart 'bout things like that. Some things I can figur' out real goodt." He was dead right. I had noticed the man coming into the library with his tutor, but had said nothing. Little escaped my friend.

He was observant and ever vigilant. He had also brought a new satchel today.

"Yep," he said, looking pleased with himself. I figur'dt that this way, no one couldt see what I hadt w'th me 'n I couldt keep them things you give me in here." He lowered his voice, earnestly somber as he glanced around. "I gotta be careful from now on out. I do not want *no one* 'ta knowt why we was here 'n what it was we was doin'.""

Protection of this man's secret was paramount, his primary focus. I knew this from Day One. As we walked into the library that first morning, me smiling at people and speaking, I immediately sensed that Roy Caddell would have liked to have sunk into the cracks of the concrete. Never to be noticed.

"I'M ASHAM'DT I CAIN'T READ 'N WRITE — NOT JIST A LITTLE BIT, BUT A WHOLE LOT SHAMEFUL. MY GREAT FEAR ALL MY LIFE IS PEOPLE FINDIN' OUT. IT'S A BIG DEAL TA ME, 'N IT PROB-LY AL-WAYS WILL BE. I CALL IT MY PER-MANENT SCAR'DT-A-PHOBIA."

Whenever we encountered others, he hung back, instinctively turning his head. He literally withered, as though he wished we were no longer together. His silent eyes pleaded: *"Do not introduce me. Do not include me, Trude. Oh, please. Pretend you do not know me."* His pain was real.

Those early months, this man moved with shoulders slumped, neck forward, head down — like a crooked finger. I felt I was dragging dead weight. It was as though he felt he had a red neon sign on his forehead that flashed: *"I cannot read. I cannot read. . . ."* It was heartbreaking.

The third lesson I had what I thought was a simple surprise for my new friend. I never dreamed the Pandora's Box I was opening. I only knew I was potentially on risky ground. This was not in my teacher's text.

"I found something yesterday that I want to see if you can read. I think you can." With that I brought out a tiny, colorful booklet of Walt Disney's classic tale, *The Fox and the Hound*. It was absolutely full of enchanting pictures and looked like it would be fun to read, regardless of age.

Roy looked startled, but eagerly took the proffered booklet and began to read. Tentatively, I will grant you; but, nonetheless, he read. I think Walt Disney himself would have been elated had he been sitting there watching us. His smile would have been as bright as mine.

> *"One sunny morning, Big Mama the owl looked down from her*
> *pitch high above the forest. Suddenly, something caught her eye.*
> *It was a little ball of bright red fur hiding in the tall grass below."*

"We stopped there, at the bottom of the first page and went over the fact that the word PITCH was really the word PERCH. He had extreme difficulty pronouncing it.

"Let's look at this word and sound it out. Watch the way my lips and my mouth make the beginning sound PER-CH." Slowly I repeated and enunciated the word: "PER-CH. PERCH."

"Remember the word CHART from the top of our workbook pages the last two days? Well, PERCH has the same -CH sound. The two words are really a lot alike: -CH, -CH, -CH." Again I enunciated, "CH-art. CHart. Chart. Per-CH. PerCH. Perch. Now you say it, Roy, and pay particular attention to the -CH sound at the end. I want to hear it!"

"Perrr-*ch*," he labored to say, for he had been watching. And listening.

"Again," I urged.

"Perr-ch."

"Again."

"Peeerr-ch."

Each time was different. Slowly he got it, after a fashion. But it was extremely difficult.

That -CH sound, coupled with the R sound, was very hard for Roy to make with his mouth. I did not know why. I could only guess that these were sounds he had never pronounced correctly before, because he had never *heard* them said accurately, distinctly. For his sake, and all that lay ahead, I felt he must learn to enunciate words he would henceforth be learning, to the very best of his abilities. Beginning now. I cut him no slack.

Much later, he confided to me, "I jist never heardt 'em saidt that way befor', Trude. That's jist the way I was grow'dt up."

"I LEARN'DT IT LIKE I HEARDT IT. ONCE'T I SAID'T IT THAT WAY A FEW YEARS, I THOUGHT I WAS RIGHT. IT MAKES SENSE 'TA ME THAT IF Y'UR TAUGHT BY THE DUMB, Y'UR GONNA BE DUMB. I DIN'T KNOW 'BOUT THAT STORE-BOUGHT TALK."

We continued reading each page of the Disney story slowly, carefully, stopping in appropriate places to go over every word that caused him trouble. There were a number: FLUTTERED, DECLARED, WIGGLED, WAGGED, INTRO-DUCED, CURIOUS, CANINE, RESPONDED, CONTINUED, ROLLICK, ROMPED, PROMISED, MEAN, ORNERY, CONFESSED, CONFUSED, CONFIDED, DETERMINED, STUBBORNLY, DECIDED, FRIGHTENED, COMMOTION, FERO-CIOUS, LURED, ONTO, DANGEROUS, CRASH-ING, HURLING, TIRED, HURT, PROTECT, UNDERSTANDING, MEANING. And FRIEND-SHIP. Yes, I mean Roy Caddell had trouble pronouncing these words, either in full or in part. We repeated each one that gave him trouble until he had each basically right; until he was reasonably comfortable saying every word. It was a time-consuming, mind-boggling, laborious process. I never could have imagined such difficulty. The word ROMPED was truly the hardest word Roy Caddell ever had to pronounce. It threw him, every single time. He could not make his mouth form that one word without considerable difficulty.

Rs often are extremely hard for nonreaders who, in general, tend to throw in Rs when they are not there — and leave them out when they are. This I observed time and again with Roy, and have since heard other tutors say the same.

Before our third session ended, I gave him three more words to pronounce and practice together so that he could feel his mouth and lips making the difficult R sound: RAMP, RUMP, ROMP. It did not take long to get two out of three, but that third one nearly did him in.

It was not until weeks later that he could pronounce "our favorite word," as we came to call it. Until that time, whenever I asked Roy to pronounce ROMP, he had to bring whatever he was doing to a full stop in order to focus his entire being on that one word.

It was an unforgettable learning experience, for both of us. Fortunately, we still laugh about it.

Slowly, we wound our way through thirteen short pages of the Disney tale, pages of words and colorful pictures that together told an enchanting story. Many words he had never read, but some he knew or we figured out, together. He was overjoyed with each effort expended, and his sizable accomplishment. He deserved to be.

"Roy, I want you to notice something about these words and this story that you might never have thought of in conjunction with reading. None of these words are worth anything alone. They are just words.

"What makes these words special and take on meaning — and begin to tell a story, is the simple fact that each word works to help another. Words are like family or love. Neither is worth anything by itself. They need each other. We all need each other. Words are no exception. We always come back to Square One, helping one another."

"I likes that," he quietly said as he looked up, startled. "But I'da shore never thought 'bout it that way. Makes sense't."

It was a simplistic correlation that had suddenly come to mind. I had to reach this man, where he was. I had become acutely aware how I had taken simple reading and writing for granted. I had never given the matter one thought until this man graphically painted the world from another perspective. It was not a pretty picture.

We went back over the Disney story another time and sounded out the harder words again. He got most right the first time.

Next, we clapped these trouble words out as we broke them into syllables. This simple clapping helped Roy realize there is a natural division to words in the English language, a pattern, rhythm. Because most words can be said in a "sing, song" cadence, the rhythm concept would be particularly important in the days that lay ahead. There was a solid reason for everything we did.

Again, we looked for Words Within Words. We talked about the fact that some of the harder words were really just simple words with different endings tacked onto them, and therefore carried slightly different meanings in this particular story. I placed my hands over parts of certain words so that Roy could see the smaller words tucked inside. Finally, the lightbulb switched on.

"A lotta them wordts I'm havin' trouble w'th here haf them endin' things on 'em you toldt me 'bout. Otherwise, I mighta knowt 'em myself." He was grinning. Me, too. I was encouraged.

Next, I read the tiny booklet out loud to him, asking him to pay close attention to the sound of my voice, the high and low tones, the pitch. I then explained that these sound variations are called "inflection," or "voice intonation. It simply means reading with feeling, Roy."

"Oh."

Then I explained that what I wanted him to hear this time was not so much the words in the story, but the tone of my voice. I told him why.

"STARTIN' OUT, MY VOICE WAS LIKE TALKIN' IN A STRAIGHT LINE. IF YA CAIN'T READT 'N WRITE, YA CAIN'T STAY IN TUNE — 'N YA SHORE CAIN'T SING BASS OR TENOR. I WAS FLAT."

"A person's reading voice is a dead giveaway that you don't read well. Beginning readers tend to read everything in a flat voice with no expression to their words and, therefore, with little meaning. It's as if you are *talking dead*. It will give you away, Roy — every single time." He nodded, as I added that "this lack of tone or pitch variation in any reader's voice is called a 'monotone.'"

He well understood the concept. It was not a hard idea for him to grasp, but it was a terribly hard one for him to do. It was years before he began to read with any real expression to his voice. He does not do this easily today.

"We're real-ly on 'ta somethin' here," he said tapping the table excitedly as I finished reading. "This here is somethin' I miss'dt 'n I knowt I need'ta get. This here is what I want ya 'ta teach me. I don't care how slow we haf'ta go 'r how long it takes. I want us 'ta keep goin' jist like we are."

The door at the end of a very long tunnel had cracked open. Roy Caddell could see light. He could see hope. I would take it any way it came.

I ended the lesson by asking *him* to read the entire Disney story over again out loud to me. I wanted him to clearly see that what he had done once, he could do again. Only this time, he could read with less hesitancy and more confidence. We had gone long on time, but I wanted this circle complete, no loose ends. I wanted him to see and feel for himself the giant step forward he had made today. He began again.

> *"One sunny morning, Big Mama the owl. . . . They were sure they would always be the very best of friends."*

As he finished, he slowly removed his glasses and turned to me, his eyes twinkling as he realized his accomplishment was no fluke. He had sailed through with flying colors. I was overjoyed. My gamble had paid off.

"Well!" I exclaimed. "What do you think?"

He sat for the longest time, just shaking his head and holding his glasses, grinning the whole while from ear to ear like the Cheshire Cat. Perhaps he was remembering where he had been, perhaps reflecting on where he was going. His entire demeanor had transformed sharply. He was another person, a human being with pride.

"We done goodt here," he flatly stated. "'N I like'dt doin' it, that's the part I don't hardt-ly understandt. Yet. This here story had lottsa them hardt wordts in it, Trude. I cain't right-ly believe I done this. Boy howdy, haf I gots me somethin 'ta tell when I gits home tonight." He was aglow, like the town square on Christmas Eve, when the switch is finally flipped on for the shimmering lights.

Roy Caddell had done a dynamite job indeed, stumbling over few words this second reading. His was an amazing accomplishment for only two hours work. He seemed to remember so many small things I was telling him. From outward appearances, this man desperately wanted to learn. That was the key to all we ever did, all we ever accomplished. He earned every step he took the hard way, *one word at a time.*

Startling as it now seems in retrospect, I brought this tiny Disney booklet to Roy for two reasons — one tangible, the other intangible.

One. This man had never read a story, not even to himself. And certainly, he had "never readt anythin' out loudt befor' comin' down here."

Two. People often live up to the expectations of others. Positives or negatives. I wanted him to know I had total confidence in his abilities to learn this, and whatever else followed. Time and again I would tell him, "You can do this!" To an outsider, I must have sounded like a broken record, or a pure simpleton.

Self-confidence is always lacking in those who do not read. This characteristic had been stressed in literacy tutoring classes. Constantly nonreaders berate themselves, often over nothing. But always, over how "dumb" they are because they cannot read. That is how they *feel.* I desperately wanted

"I DID NOT HAF ANY SELF-CONFIDENCE IN MY ED-UCASHUN. I HADT SELF-CONFI-DENCE IN MANUAL THINGS. BUT THINGS LIKE NUMBERS 'N WRITIN' 'N READIN', THAT PART I TRIED'TA HIDE. I WANT'DTA KEEP IT QUIET 'N SECRET THAT I COULDN'T DO THEM THINGS. I WAS HURTING, 'N DIN'T EVEN KNOW IT."

Roy Caddell to feel better about himself and his immense, innate capabilities. I am sure every tutor feels this way with every student they ever have.

From my limited vantage point, here was a grown man who vitally needed someone outside his own immediate family to believe in him, and to tell him so. I guess I designated myself as that person.

The Fox and the Hound is still in Roy's possession, dated May 9, 1994, with both our signatures on the last page. A "keeper" as my husband would say.

THE PRINTED WORD

*"I wanna readt a paper so's I don't al-ways haf'ta rely
on somebod' else'ta git my news, 'r on that telly-vision.
I'm smart e'nuff 'ta knowt they jist give ya what they
wants ya 'ta hear anyways."*

By our fourth lesson, we were meeting Monday, Wednesday and Friday mornings from straight up nine o'clock until eleven. As the weeks turned into months, we stayed until noon. We never planned to meet that long each day, it simply worked out that way. He was so anxious to learn. I was so anxious to teach.

Initially, Roy Caddell would have come five days a week for lessons, had it been possible for me. I know most tutors meet weekly with their students, usually for an hour or so each time. Such was rarely the case with us.

The man did not seem to tire in our sessions, and I was staying alert to this very real possibility. Our lessons were long. He had myriad responsibilities elsewhere. He never looked at his watch or seemed hurried, or to appear to crave a cigarette. It was as if time stood still for us during those three hours. It was surreal.

We had run into one slight problem. Roy was not studying the words I sent home with him. I was not sure how to handle this, simply because he was making such a concerted effort in class. I did not want to squelch him. He was still sensitive, and very tentative. His feet were not yet on solid ground.

Turns out this slight problem took care of itself. Early one morning we happened to run into Delia Brown, the area literacy coordinator and a good friend. She was sharp, intuitive, caring and very familiar with Roy's case. They chatted briefly before she both asked and stated, "I know you must be doing your homework?"

"Well, no, ma'am. Not, yet. I'm awful busy all the time at home. I's got an awful lots 'ta do now." And he impishly grinned. She did not.

"Well," and Delia paused, looking him dead in the eye, "for you to get the most out of this, Roy, and help yourself, you *must* spend at least twenty minutes a day going over what you have covered in your lessons each time you meet. You *must* do your homework."

End of sermon. End of problem. Both accomplished with a soft voice and no hurt feelings. Yes! I just smiled my thanks like a contented cat and did not mention homework again for months.

Roy came prepared thereafter, too prepared initially. There was little for me to correct on those early papers of his. I was amazed. I was also naive. What I was seeing on his papers did not match what he was struggling desperately to read in lessons. His homework reflected more advanced skills than he showed on a daily basis, as he labored to pronounce, and then correctly write, every word. There was a vital missing link.

Suddenly it dawned on me! Roy was getting help at home from either his wife or his son. I should have known. But why? Why was it now so important for him to bring a corrected text back to me? Finally, I had to ask him pointblank.

"Roy, did you actually spell all these words? By yourself? Because something isn't matching up here."

"Uh, no," he said sheepishly. "Not real-ly. The ones I warn't too shore 'bout, well, I ask'dt my wife 'n she helpt me. So's I'd haf it right when I gotta class *'n you'd see how smart I was*," and he grinned with pure self-satisfaction at his cleverness.

"Roy. You are plenty smart, of that there is no doubt. But, we have got to make a deal. Certainly your wife can help you, but I cannot if I do not know where you need help. From these papers, it looks like you know everything. That is not at all accurate from our class reading. You cannot read in class many of the words that I see written correctly on these last homework papers.

"There is a puzzle piece missing here. What that boils down to, is that you are cheating yourself if you do not need my help." He looked at me and grinned, knowing he had been caught with his hand in the cookie jar. In point of fact, his case had been one of pure self-defense. *The man did not want to look dumb!*

Thereafter, he devised his own system for telling me where he need-ed help, when he had doubt — for alerting me to the times when he had asked for and received help from his wife or son. He began to underline any word he had written out as homework, but did not know how to spell himself.

It was a brilliant compromise that produced some absolutely hilarious homework papers that "led't us 'roundt the worldt in my lif'time."

To our fourth lesson, I again brought cards to add to the growing list of words Roy knew and could read and recognize easily. If we used an unusual word in class conversations — and back then, most were — I made a card for it. "That's what I like best. Them little cardts."

Because the Walt Disney story had so many words with varied endings, I continued on this bent. His antennae were up, focused. I did not want his attentions to stray. I began introducing words that were not in our text, but words I had heard him use in conversations. We started slowly.

Words like BARELY, NAMED, FRIENDLY, SAFELY, LIGHTLY, LOVELY, BRIGHTLY, RARELY and HAPPILY, which I saved until last. They were all words with different endings and, in the case of HAPPI-LY, slightly different spellings. We read and pronounced each carefully.

We went over the beginning sounds for each word, and discussed how some of the words were similar in both pronunciation and spelling. Then I covered up the endings on each to help Roy see the original root words before the endings had been added.

"Oh, yeah. I r'member what you toldt me 'bout endings." He hesitated. I waited. "They meant, that the wordt means a little somethin' differ'nt." He looked pleased with himself.

Next, I covered up various parts of each word as we looked for Words Within Words. Roy liked to do this and was getting dern good at it. Sometimes, he even saw those small words before I did, which always tickled him. This was fun, not work for either of us.

Slowly, he was gaining another much needed skill through the introduction of everyday words outside our text. In addition, he was gaining much needed confidence in one more area of this complex maze of language, through repetition. Crucial.

"Now, Roy, the reason I included HAPPILY in this listing is because I want you to be aware that not all words are changed simply by tacking different endings onto them. Some words, such as the root word HAPPY, are first changed in their spelling. In the case of HAPPILY, from the story of *The Fox and the Hound,* we must change the Y to an I before adding -LY. *And we must do this every single time. Absolutely no exceptions."*

"So that's why I seen that wordt that way, but I never knowt why. Hmmm. I'da never figger'dt that out 'bout a wordt if you hadn't show'dt me, 'n it's somethin' I need'ta know."

"Yes, you do. I would be most unfair if I did not point out the exceptions to what we do. That is the complexity of the English language, Roy. It is hard to learn, almost cruel at times. Certainly, we will cover each of these oddities as we come to them; but in the meantime, you need to be aware of some of these things."

"I shore do." He shook his head in growing awareness and recognition of just where he was. He was pensive.

"I knowt I haf a long ways 'ta go, Trude. But then," he said brightening, "I think we've come pret-ty far al-readt'. I feel real goodt 'bout this. We're goin' down the right track, I'm shore a that."

In the stories that accompanied lessons, we had come across different punctuation marks, and even the possessive case. The story in today's lesson featured quotation marks.

In preparation, I had brought a long piece of cardboard on which I had printed all the various punctuation marks down its length. I had used a magic marker so each example stood out sharply. Roy had never seen all these marks together. Before our lessons, he never had known of their existence.

(On this card, I made a dreadful mistake. I am a terrible speller and I wrote Explanation Mark instead of Exclamation Mark. "Something does not look right here, Roy." When my error finally dawned on me later that night, I promptly called him. We laughed, but it really was no laughing

"I WOULDN'T A GIVE A NICKLE F'R ALL THEM MARKS WHEN WE START'DT OUT, THEY DIN'T MEAN NUTHIN' 'TA ME. IN MY WHOLE LIFE, I NEVER HADT ANY USE F'R THEM COMMAS 'N A-POSTROPHES. NOW I KNOWT THEY'RE THE SAME THING, ONLY ONE'S UP 'N ONE'S DOWN. IT'S LIKE A PUZZLE, I MAY NOT BE ABLE 'TA DO IT — BUT I WANT ALL THE PIECES."

matter. Especially when, for weeks thereafter, he said "ex-planation mark." Horrors.)

On this same essential card, I wrote that "Book titles are underlined," <u>The Bible</u> was my example; and that the "Proper names of people, places and things begin with a capital letter, such as Roy, Muskogee Library and Laubach Literacy Program." His eyebrows went up.

"Well, I'll be," he said. "That's why I seen 'em that way, like on telly-vision. But I never knowt why."

Handing him the long punctuation card to take home, I told him that, "believe it or not, in time these will become like old and trusted friends to you, which will be great." He looked dubious.

"Trude, I knowt I need'ta knowt sum'a this. This here explains a whole lotta things I seen befor' 'n never understoodt. I knowt I will use it. I jist don't knowt 'x-actly when." He grinned at his own satire.

Roy had previously told me that he had learned many things from television game shows, such as *Wheel of Fortune*. I did not know this. Basically, I loathe television, but it obviously had some positives. Not once did Roy mention watching children's television shows to learn to read, which honestly surprised me when I thought about it objectively.

Referring back to the punctuation list from which we were working, I pointed to the -AL in the word, CAPITAL. Here was another "logical progression" that was out of my mouth before I could catch it.

"Roy, if we change just one letter in this word, the A to an O at the end of the word Capital, we would have a totally different word with a totally different meaning." His eyes opened wide and he quickly moved his chair closer to the table to better see exactly what I was showing him.

"C-A-P-I-T-<u>O</u>-L," I both spelled out loud and wrote down for him, "refers to a building. Either the capitol building of the State of Oklahoma or any state — or to the capitol building of our nation's capital in Washington, D.C.

"Whereas the word C-A-P-I-T-<u>A</u>-L," and I spelled it out slowly to emphasize the letter A, "refers to money, or a capital letter of the alphabet, or to the seat of any government, such as 'The CAPIT<u>A</u>L of Oklahoma is Oklahoma City; The CAPIT<u>A</u>L of Texas is Austin; The CAPIT<u>A</u>L of the United States is Washington, D.C.'

"But — and this is the tricky part, Roy — the building where our state Legislature meets in our state CAPIT<u>A</u>L in Oklahoma City to decide state laws is called a CAPIT<u>O</u>L. Spelled with an O. -OL." He looked shocked. "I know, Roy. It absolutely makes no sense. *It just is.*

"The reason I mention this is because we can do this with any number of words in our English language: *Totally change their meaning by changing just one letter.*" His eyes were riveted to the paper. He was barely breathing, as was I.

He had listened intently to all I had said. How much he retained, I did not know. I only knew that I would never insult this man by silently insinuating that he could not comprehend several factors of our complex language at once. He could. Finally, he softly responded.

"Alotta this will prob-ly stick w'th me on down the years. I'll r'member it 'n it'll helpt me. Right now, it's not too bright in my mindt. But, I think I'm smart e-nuff so's I can write one big wordt 'n haf lottsa little wordts in it. It takes time f'r me. It's slow. But, boy howdy. I shore din't knowt what one little ole letter couldt do. It's amazin'." So, too, was this man.

In his mind, all this was hard. Hard as in complicated, complex — but not impossible. He was looking for a way, any way, to simplify what I was trying to teach him, what he so desperately was trying to learn. From his vantage point, what he was now attempting must have seemed unreachable. Yet, he persevered. I often thought it miraculous he did not quit. I felt for him, but at the same time, I realized that he would do whatever it took to accomplish what he set out to do. The man impressed me.

We covered much new ground on that fourth day. The assigned new words were: RIVER, SNAKE, TENT, VALLEY, WOMAN and YELLS.

"YA HANDL'DT THIS BRILLIANTLY. YA TOLDT ME YOU WERE LEARNIN', TOO. YA NEVER MADE'T ME FEEL STUPID. YA KEPT THROWIN' IN ALL THE TIME 'BOUT HOW SMART I WAS. I KNEW BETTER, BUT I LIK'DT HEARIN' IT. I'M HAPPY W'TH THE LEARNIN' YOU'VE TAUGHT ME, TRUDE. I'M NOT WANTIN'TA GIT TO THE TOP, I JIST WANNA GIT IN LINE."

"Ugh!" Roy exclaimed. "I wish they'dt pick'dt some other wordt besides snake 'ta teach us. I hate snakes! But, guns — well now, I like guns. I wish they'dt give us some wordts I like'dt." We both laughed, but I remembered his plea.

This day, as before, each of our new words was accompanied by a corresponding picture and story. Again, I had made flash cards for each.

Roy went through this lesson "like high water over low land." He never missed a beat as he forged ahead, snakes and all.

We were instructed at this juncture to practice our printing. For Roy Caddell, that meant cursive writing. For me, that meant "good luck." As we worked on his penmanship, we laughed about mine.

When I wrote out sentences or words for him, he often teasingly said, "Hmm. I cain't hardt-ly make this out." Or, "Ya do needt help, Trude." Or, "Ya shore that's what this says here?"

This certainly was not the first time anyone had told me my handwriting left a lot to be desired — gorgeous, but nearly impossible to read. Oddly enough, I never dreamed that my penmanship would enter into all of this. Foolish me, how did I think Roy was going to learn? By osmosis?

My writing was legendary — as in, not good. I told Roy of the time I was at the hospital and was introduced to a man who worked at the post office. He slowly repeated my name, stroking his chin. Finally, he exclaimed, "Trude Norman! I know who you are. You're the lady with the writing we can't none of us read." True story. And a good joke I have told on myself a thousand times. Roy loved it.

When it came to penmanship, his greatest need in those early lessons was to relax and build confidence in his own abilities. Ultimately, Roy Caddell

FROM DAY ONE, ROY CADDELL DESPERATELY WANTED TO LEARN THAT "FANCY WRITIN' THEM OTHER PEOPLE USE." PRINTING WAS NEVER A PRIMARY FOCUS FOR HIM. CURSIVE WRITING ALWAYS WAS. EACH WORD HE WROTE INCREASED HIS ORAL AND WRITTEN VOCABULARIES. WRITING WORDS WAS CRUCIAL FOR THIS MAN. HE LITERALLY LEARNED *ONE WORD AT A TIME.*

had a legible hand. He worked diligently at home, which was tremendously helpful to me. That way, I could easily correct his words and letters, which were primitive initially. He truly liked practicing his penmanship, "'specially since'dt I'm not so nervous now as I was at first."

Perhaps because of my own limitations, I wanted this man to be acutely aware that not all letters are made the same. Each has a distinct shape. It does make a difference how every letter is made! Beautiful penmanship is highly respected in many countries.

Roy labored at moving his hand freely as he wrote. He never had done this as an adult. It was tedious. It was imperative that he get the rounded parts of certain letters correct: the a, b, c, d, g, m, n, o, p. He had to practice that some letters fill most of the space on a line: b, d, f, h, k, l; while others are written on the line, but also extend below: g, j, p.

His student workbook was helpful with printing exercises. It gave examples of the lower case letters we had been given to date. Each letter was presented in block form on simulated wide-lined paper. Each writing line in Roy's workbook had a light green dotted line printed down the middle of each line-space. This faint dotted line served as a visual guide when Roy printed his letters, and later when he incorporated cursive.

The workbook also showed precisely how each letter is made, so that a student can trace and practice letters in his or her own spare time.

But Roy's greatest aid, without doubt, was his wife. Hazel Caddell writes well and is quite intelligent. She helped her husband immensely. She was by far his most valuable asset, and he knew it.

I thought Roy wrote incredibly well for someone who had not gone to school "much past the sev'nth 'r eighth grade. I cain't real-ly r'member too well. I jist r'member I was pret-ty big when I fi-nally stopp'dt goin'."

Not once during that first year did I ever hear him say he had "quit school." I only knew he had discontinued his schooling when he was a mere thirteen-year-old boy, a boy who too soon became a man.

It seemed to me that Roy had not completed the eighth grade. I vividly remember that year as being the absolute hardest of all my years in school — including college — especially in math and English. Both were killers for me. I did poorly in math, I excelled in English.

A large part of my job with Roy Caddell was to listen. His primary goal on our first day of lessons was to be able to read a daily newspaper.

"So's I don't al-ways haf'ta rely on somebod' else'ta git my news, 'r on that telly-vision. I'm smart e'nuff 'ta knowt they jist give ya what they wants ya 'ta hear anyways."

As we were walking downstairs two days ago, I had stopped to show him where various newspapers from across our country were kept at the Muskogee Public Library. I wanted him to be aware that many, many items besides books are found in public libraries across America. He was fascinated, and surprised. On this day, I wanted him to realize, in part, a personal goal.

"OK, Roy. This morning I have brought a newspaper. Will you please read this main headline to me?"

His eyes opened wide as I pulled out the front page of our daily paper the morning after Oklahoma had defeated the lottery. The headline was huge, almost two inches tall, and read: ALL BETS OFF! It was a fabulous learning tool.

"You want me 'ta readt this?" he asked incredulously, pulling out his glasses as he moved his chair nearer to the table. I looked around the room to insinuate that there was no one else there.

"Yes. You."

He easily read the headline to both of us, although he was in disbelief that he could actually be reading a newspaper. I loved watching his face as all this unfolded. His sheer joy was my privilege.

For the rest of that day, we went over different aspects of that paper. I showed him the masthead and title; where the date and the page numbers are; how he can find where a story is continued; the want ads; where the sports are and how to find scores of yesterday's major league games; where to find rainfall to date, or how high the area rivers are. And I explained the photo captions, or writing under pictures.

I pointed out the different sections of the paper, and where each is labeled Section A, Section B, Section C, and so on. Each section typically carries a different type of news, such as world news, local news, sports and business news, and classifieds and comics. When news is divided into smaller and more manageable sections, I told him, it is easier to find a specific subject or interest.

Roy loved it. He never took his glasses off. This was fun for me, I adore anything that has to do with newspapers. Years ago, after receiving my journalism degree from the University of Oklahoma, I had edited a small weekly paper. Black ink runs in my veins. My day is never complete without reading at least two daily newspapers.

Maybe now, Roy would at least *touch* one.

By the time we finished that paper, reading bits and pieces here and there, with Roy doing minimal reading to me, he was more at ease with a paper. This was critical for him, "since'dt befor', I wouldn't hardt-ly pick up one a them newspapers. It wouldn't do me no goodt anyways 'cause I couldn't readt nuthin'." He noted my quizzical look.

"I'm serious, Trude," he emphatically stated. "On this here I din't take no chances! If ever I was out somewheres of a mornin' havin' coffee, 'n even kinder lookin' at one a them newspapers — if I seent someone comin' in who might sit down close 'ta me — well, I put that paper down real quick like befor' they maybe couldt a seen me lookin' at it; 'n then them come 'n sit down by me 'n ask me what it was I was a readin' in that paper.

"Or maybe, if they'da seen me w'th a newspaper in my handt, they coulda triedt'ta come up 'n talk'ta me 'bout the news a the day, 'r somethin' else't *they'dt* readt in that paper. I tell ya, on this here *I din't take no chances!* I left them newspapers alone!"

Roy Caddell never paused for breath while he stated his case. He kept jabbing that conference table angrily, as if to release years of torment on that immobile object. I can still see him.

His raw tone suddenly made me acutely aware of the searing pain of living a lie. Much negative energy and constant tactical maneuvering go daily into such hardship and pretension.

Somehow, I had to try and neutralize this obvious negative for my friend. I heard only resignation in his voice, and abject despair. I still hear him beating that table. The image is burned in my memory.

"There is one thing I want you always to keep in mind here, Roy — not only about newspapers, but about other things as well. Most of the world operates on the printed word. Not on that 'fancy writing' you mentioned on our first day. I mean, the simplest form of writing in our known world. Words printed as they are still being taught to children in grade schools across our nation. Words you can come to read and understand easily for yourself, by yourself." He looked up sharply, now vitally interested.

"All of our books and magazines and newspapers are in this simplistic printed form; all of our road signs — like STOP; all our billboards; student textbooks and workbooks; *The Bible;* movie titles; grocery listings above aisles in supermarkets; ads in the newspapers; cookbooks and labels on food.

"Labels on clothing; directional signs in stores; gas station locations; street names; maps; hymnals; packaging directions; the alphabet; menus; television and movie schedules. All typewriters and computers use printed letters. All dictionaries are printed, as are manual instructions, and every single book every written!

"Every solitary one of these things comes to us in our daily lives through the printed word, Roy — our language in its simplest and most basic form.

"So, you just remember that you are going to be able to read a whole lot more than you ever dreamed possible, faster than you ever thought possible. You remember that what you are practicing and learning right now is going to serve you well the rest of your life.

"You are going to be able to operate very well, thank you, in the World of the Printed Word, Mr. Caddell. Very well indeed." A simmering smile crossed his well-lined face. He began to relax.

This was a concept he never once had considered. Nor had I. Some things we take for granted, they simply are. This was one. Roy shook his head in disbelief until slowly, the dawning realization that *maybe,* just *maybe* he could do this after all took root in his mind.

Finally, he quietly said, "I'dt shore never thought a it that way befor'. Not ever. *Maybe* I will be able 'ta do this. Maybe I will. But, I still haf a might-y long ways 'ta go."

"Yes, you do. But, we all do, Roy, in one area of our lives or another, although some people never realize or admit that they need help. They think that they have all the answers. No one does. You are very wise to have realized your great need to learn to read and write. I admire you."

"Trude. I thank ya f'r that, but I'dt shore trade't you sum'a my wisdom f'r sum'a y'ur ed-ucashun."

"Understandable, Sir. If we humans were really as wise as we think we are, no one's education would ever stop. I am still learning. You are still learning. Knowledge is out there awaiting us all. We only have to reach out and grab it.

"That is why there are dictionaries, why there are libraries. Think of the people we see here, day after day after day. They come needing help. They come searching for answers.

"That is why you are here, why you come so faithfully. And why, my friend, I hold the highest esteem for you." I reached out to touch his arm as I smiled.

"I'm gladt I came today," he said, turning. "I need'dt this. It's been a real-ly goodt lesson. Thank you."

Roy Caddell went home that day with Encouragement. They made a handsome pair.

At this juncture of study, this man had learned to read and recognize eighteen different words. Each word had as its beginning letter, a different letter of the alphabet. Thus, Roy Caddell now knew eighteen different letters of the alphabet, albeit in no particular order.

He was oblivious of this fact; he was not counting, but I was. I said nothing.

We were about to close in on his major deficit — and his greatest joy.

"I shore do!" he quickly answered. "But, do you have time? I knowt you have more im-port'nt things 'ta do than this here."

"No, Roy, I do not."

In truth, nothing was more important to me than our learning this. Together. I was overjoyed for my friend; and overcome by his ebullience with such a simple concept — one I had taken for granted my whole life. His childlike joy humbled me.

We jumped ahead to Lesson Five and quickly read the six new words: BOX, ZIPPER, QUARTER, SHOP, CHILDREN and THANK. With these words, Roy would learn the final letters of that mysterious alphabet.

First we tackled SHOP, CHILDREN and THANK. I wanted to end our lesson with the three missing letters, so I saved BOX, ZIPPER and QUARTER until last.

These first three words, SHOP, CHILDREN and THANK, introduced us to "consonant blends" and "digraphs."

I calmly told him that "the blending of -SH and -CH are called consonant blends. The letters -TH are consonants, but their sounds are called digraphs — which are two-letter combinations that make only one sound. These are tricky, Roy, but they are manageable. You can do this." He merely nodded and never took his eyes off the page.

"These sounds may be held a long time, too, Roy, just as the short vowel sounds. SHHHHop, CHHHHildren, THHHHank."

Ultimately, he was able to enunciate each of these words correctly, but they were difficult for him to pronounce. Each worked his muscles and caused him to twist his mouth and jaws in laborious contortions.

Glossing over and slurring words and sounds was not in my game plan. Roy Caddell had to work more than just his writing hand and his brain each time he came to class. He had to work his being.

The -CH sound we had touched upon already, in the word CHART from the workbook lessons, as well as the troublesome word PERCH from the Walt Disney story. He certainly remembered that one. Today's focus had the -CH sound situated at the beginning of a word. He understood.

The -SH and -CH letter combinations Roy Caddell could tolerate, even accept. The -TH digraph soon would be at the top of his all-time Do Not Like list! He loathed -TH, "'cause it makes ab-solutely no sens't, when you cain't hear but one'a them!" I could not argue with his logic.

The digraphs -WH and -PH, as in WHISTLE, PHYSICIAN and TELEPHONE, soon would make that same reprehensible list. To this day, Roy still talks about "all them wordts. They're the worst."

The one thing he needed to know about the word QUARTER was that "the letter Q is always followed by the letter U. No exceptions. Grade-schoolers today learn that the two letters are 'married.' But, please, hand me your dictionary so we can be sure this is true."

"Well, I'da never knowt that," he remarked as we scanned every Q word in his small pocket dictionary. "I ain't never been in the Q part of a dict-shunary befor'." True, but he had never "been't inside't a dict-shunary" period before our lessons.

Every lesson for years thereafter, we seized opportunities to use his. When we could not find a word in his small dictionary, we used the huge one in the library, just outside our room. Our efforts paid off. Coupled with his new-found knowledge of the alphabet, the dictionary soon became this one man's greatest tool.

Three years later he was to tell me, "Outside'a *The Bible,* Trude, that there book is the best book ev'r written. But I hate'dt them things 'ta start w'th!" Gross understatement!

Roy had absolutely no trouble with the X in BOX and the Z in ZIPPER as we went over their respective pronunciations and sounds. As I held up their word cards, he quickly recognized each. That meant that, finally, we could add the last three remaining alphabetic letters beside the other twenty-three on the lines in his yellow legal tablet.

The missing letters of that heretofore unfathomable alphabet had "come home to roost." Q, X and Z were where they belonged. Roy grinned the whole time he was writing these last letters down. So did I, just watching him.

Then I had him count, once again, to see if all twenty-six letters were really there. It did not take long.

"One, two, three, four, five, six, seven, eight, nine, ten, eleven, twelve, thirteen, fourteen, fifteen, sixteen, seventeen, eighteen, nineteen, twenty, twenty-one, twenty-two, twenty-three, twenty-four, twenty-five, twenty-six.

"Yep. I git twenty-six al-right! I jist cain't hardt-ly believe it. I cain't wait'ta git home 'n tell my wife!"

Always, I shall believe Roy Caddell floated home on Day Five, bouncing about the insides of that brown truck as he navigated the highway back to cows and family. The smile on his face as we walked out of that library was radiant, enveloping. Had I been a mouse in his pocket that night, what a celebration within that family I would have seen!

He was right. This was "our best lesson!"

Incredible as it might now seem, Roy Caddell had never asked about the alphabet prior to this lesson. The subject had never come up in conversation. He never broached the matter, as to what we were studying or where we were going with the words and concepts we were learning.

True, I casually had mentioned the alphabet on two previous occasions, but it obviously had not taken — which surprised me.

However, it is easy to look at overall conversations we had with a jaundiced eye when one is perched comfortably in the seat of education. The alphabet becomes a "given." Accepted fact. The norm.

Not so from the viewpoint of a nonreader. To them, the world looks vastly different. Such was the case with my friend. He was blindsided by my base question: "How many letters are in the alphabet?"

To find suddenly that this is a gift he, too, can have and master, is to better understand how at least 20 percent of our population lives *every single day.*

It is a scary, scary thought that deserves our compassion, our interest, our dollars, and, our greatest dedication to eradicate.

DAY
6

STUPID IS NOT A LABEL

*"I been em-barrass'dt e'nuff al-read'ty in my life. I
shore don't needt no more!"*

This day's lesson would be short. I had a responsibility in a morning meeting, which I had explained to Roy previously.

"We don't haf'ta meet," he had urged. "I don't want you 'ta get tire'dt a this 'n then not wanna come. Why don't we jist skip this one?"

"I don't want to *just not come,* Roy. I want to see how you are doing after the weekend, especially since you are going to be gone on Friday." He merely shrugged his shoulders and gave up.

Primarily, though, I wanted to set a precedent that we both stay focused on our task at hand: Teaching him to read. I knew if I made a commitment for those initial three meetings a week, he would do likewise. But first, *I* had to set the example.

He later confessed to me several times in early months, "I thought 'bout callin' you today 'n cancelin', but I knowt I need'dta come. I knowt I'dt learnt somethin'. I al-ways do."

Though our meeting was to be brief and hurried, it was nonetheless important and had purpose. There were the two items I wanted to give Roy Caddell on Day Six.

One: The letters of the alphabet on one long cardboard strip. This was the first time as an adult that he had seen all twenty-six letters in their proper sequential order. Major.

Two: I had brought a marvelous feature story, an interview, from our area newspaper about a local football coach who was retiring. I felt his words would speak to Roy.

I had highlighted in pink and green inks the parts of the clipping that I thought Roy could read. He looked surprised as I handed the paper his way. It was never his first choice to read to me. He always preferred the reverse. He reached reluctantly for his glasses and *haltingly* began to read:

"The last vacation I took was twenty-three years ago, when my daughter, who just graduated from Northeastern State University was one year old. I don't feel proud about that. I feel stupid. It's time that I do something about it."

With that, Roy pushed the article back and turned, waiting.

"You see, Roy, all of us feel stupid at times in our lives. We all make dumb choices, we do foolish things. *Everyone* makes unwise decisions. But, that does not make us stupid. Quite the reverse.

"Here is a man with at least one college degree, who is now willing to publicly admit that he made a foolish choice years ago. More importantly, he is choosing to make another choice for his life now, to make changes within himself and his thinking. To me, that makes him wise, Roy. Very, very wise.

"I have heard it said there is a vast difference between stupidity and ignorance. Stupidity can last forever. Ignorance can be temporary. I think this article applies to you. You are a wise man to have recognized your tremendous need to learn to read.

"But to be willing to come and ask for help, particularly at your age, leaves me with nothing but the greatest admiration for you. I am terribly proud of you, Mr. Caddell, and all you are doing to help yourself. That is what I wanted to tell you today."

For a long moment he sat, his thoughts far, far away. Slowly, a warm smile crept across his face as he nodded, reaching for his handkerchief. It was his turn not to be able to speak.

"OK, Friend. There is one other thing I need to tell you here, about the alphabet, that the workbook is stressing now. All the letters in the alphabet that are not vowels are called 'consonants.' *Every single one of them.*"

"You meant those A, I, O. . . . Oh, yeah, that E 'n U. And them part'-times, that there W 'n . . . ummm, Y. You meant all them other letters are called 'con-suents?'"

"Yes. I mean absolutely every other letter of that alphabet is called a consonant. Every B. Every C, every D, F, G, H, J, K, L, M, N, P, Q, R, S, T, V, X and Z. Every one. Every time."

"If you say so, I guess't I'll haf'ta r'member it. There shore is a bunch 'ta this alpha-bet letter stuff." He sounded none-too-thrilled. Maybe he thought learning would end with vowels.

"You have to remember this, Roy. There is no way around it. And you have to get the proper pronunciation, too. So let me hear you say the word CON-SO-NANT. CONSO-NANT. CONSONANT."

It was not easy. His old habits were hard to break. Once again, he was in a convoluted tongue twisting contest. I sat in utter amazement as I tried to imagine how I would say the word had I never heard it before. He did very well, considering.

"Roy, I am not telling you that you will go around saying, 'This letter is a consonant,' or 'This letter is a vowel.' You will not. I am merely telling you, you need to know the difference, and what that difference is. You also need to know how to pronounce the word reasonably well, because someday, somewhere, it will come up in conversation. You know it will. And I do not want you embarrassed. Not ever." He whirled around to face me.

"I thank ya f'r that. I been em-barrass'dt e'nuff al-read'ty in my life. I shore don't needt no more!" The warmth of his smile slowly enveloped the whole room as we gathered our things to leave.

It had been another good day. Short, but very, very good.

DAY

7

TENACITY AND PROGRESS

"All a this is still so new 'ta me that it makes me
nervous. I'm so afear'dt that I'll make me a mistake,
that I cain't hardt-ly con-centrate on learnin' how'ta
spell them wordts right now. I guess what I'm tryin'ta
tell ya is, that I'm still in the baby steps. But I'm a
goin' forwardt. That's the only'est part that counts."

From day one, Laubach workbooks had included additional words to be taught with every lesson. Subsequently, I made word cards for each. Roy carried all these back and forth to class each time. His black satchel was beginning to bulge.

These "new story words" through Lesson Six were: THIS, IS, A, THE, HAS, IN, HER, AND, MAN, GIRL'S, AT, LOOKS, AN, PICKS, HE, HIS, GIVES, TO, SHE, PUTS, GET, SELLS, FOR, HIM, THEY, BOY, SAYS and YOU.

The addition of twenty-eight "new story words" was helpful to Roy. Each increased his vocabulary and bolstered his word recognition skills. The base of our pyramid was solidly in place, and going upward, one block at a time.

My grave concern at this juncture was that the vital words I, WE, ME and AM were nowhere to be found in teaching materials. In actuality, they were nowhere to be found in our first workbook, except for the word AM — which was listed only in reference in the back of my workbook. The integral word, *I*, did not appear in lessons for weeks hence.

Roy Caddell initially did not know the word, *I*, even existed. He had trouble reading it, he made a guess. The first time he wrote, *I*, from class dictation, was with a lower case letter. I was shocked. Too many basic words of the English language do not exist for these people. Tragically sad.

Of the four words concerning me now, only three — I, WE and ME — were included in the list of "300 Most Frequently Used Words." *But,*

ONE WORD AT A TIME   51

nowhere was AM to be found! From my perspective, this was startling. No person can long operate without the verb To Be.

The bottom line remained that Roy Caddell could not operate without I, WE, ME and AM. I had a choice: Include them or leave him hanging. I chose inclusion.

Lesson Six today was to cover paragraphs and capital letters when used with names.

In our first lesson, we had studied that every sentence begins with a capital letter. Somehow that day, I had sensed Roy did not know this, but I was never certain and I did not ask. My own teacher's text never mentioned this basic premise. Surely, I must have overlooked it.

I simply told Roy that very first day that, "Beginning every sentence with a capital letter is a must. No exceptions." Then I made sure he did it. Over time, he told me he had not even known this "f'r pos'tive."

On Day Seven, the jarring fact remained that Roy Caddell had yet to ascertain that *all* proper names begin with a capital letter. He wrote his own that way from memory and years of practice. From perforce. But, he did not know why. To my surprise, he had no idea that capital letters applied to other people's names as well.

He did not initially write my name with a capital, he used all lower case letters. I was taken aback.

Once I softly explained that, "It takes a capital T, Roy," he quickly understood. His immediate reply was standard, as was disgust with himself over having missed it. "A course'dt. I'm sorry. I shouldn't haf done it."

Not so. Capital letters held absolutely no meaning for Roy *outside of his own immediate family circle.* That long-ago punctuation card had read "Roy." It had not read "Sally" or "Sam" or "Mike Norman."

Though he did not know this essential tenet originally, it was the one that he most easily adopted and applied. Once I pointed out the principle, he rarely missed capitalizing a proper name thereafter. If he did, he quickly caught and corrected his own mistake, a mistake he made for two reasons:

One. He was not used to writing anything down.

Two. "I can-not think a all them things at onc'dt y'ur tellin' me. My pencil cain't keep up w'th my mindt. My pencil's dull 'n my mindt's not as sharp as it us'dta be."

Capitalization of proper names was a simple rule I had thought my friend would know. I was dead wrong.

Paragraphs are crucial to the English language and to the element of composition. No reader can operate without paragraphs, certainly not beginning readers. This basic principle, I hit sideways.

"Paragraphs, Roy, are like old-fashioned theater guides who help you find your seat in a darkened theatre. They show you the way. Paragraphs give vital information to the reader. Let me show you how and why." He moved his chair closer, still suspect.

On a small sheet of paper, without indentations and without a single division or break, I printed a lengthy piece of writing: Line after line after line of words and sentences, running from one edge of the page to the other. It was downright scary to look at, intimidating.

"Would you like to try and read this to me, Sir?" His eyes opened wide. I let him off the hook with a grin.

"Nor would I. I honestly thought about not including any punctuation marks on this entire page, to illustrate how this pesky Education Business is trying to help you. Punctuation marks and paragraphs want you to like them, Roy. Remember that."

He nodded, looking relieved. Then I asked him to please pull out his workbook.

We looked back over the stories we had read from Lesson One through today, and observed that, within every story, were groups of sentences. Each was divided by considerable white space between the last line of one group of sentences and the first line of the next. This white space was an important tipoff that something was changing. Stay alert.

A "white space alert" within writing might mean any number of things: A new speaker; ongoing dialogue; a new idea; special emphasis; or that the length of one paragraph was simply getting too long. Roy had not noted these helpful clues previously.

"Why, now I see why sum'a them little things 'r big 'uns. I gots'ta start payin' more at-tenshun to what y'ur sayin', 'n what it is they're showin'."

"Good idea. Keep listening, there's more. . . ." I explained how paragraphs function as distinct divisions within any writing, and how the educated world cannot operate without paragraphs.

"No book would sell without paragraphs. No newspaper. No written matter. Nothing. No one could read it. No one would want to. We all would go blind before we finally gave up. What I'm saying, Roy, is that paragraphs are nice. Paragraphs, you will like. They are on your side. New friends. Now, pronouncing paragraphs? Well, that's going to be a little harder...."

And, it was hard. Another tongue twisting contest he hated. Repeatedly, I had him pronounce the word. I still can visualize his painful efforts.

"Parrr-a-grap."

"Again."

"Paaar-ra-grap."

"Once more, and let me hear the -PH at the end. Your favorite." He did not smile.

"Par-ra-graph."

"Together now."

"Para-graph."

"And?"

"Paragraph."

"Fortunately, Roy, this word you will never have to say to any but family, or me. On this word, you will be safe. But, keep practicing on the way home." Finally, he smiled.

Before we ended our seventh session, we went over the punctuation list he had copied at home and brought to show me. He did this on his own, because he liked "them little excitin' marks."

Quickly, I zeroed in on the fact that what he read to himself and then copied, was not always what he wrote down. I had noted this in class, when he would omit or transpose letters as I dictated words he knew how to spell. When he realized his error, it frustrated him. I had to be careful here.

"Roy, please read me what you have written here, " I asked, holding his paper before him.

"Now, I want'ta be right on sayin' them wordts. It's pret-ty im-port'nt. I can talk all day long, but if you do not understandt me, it don't do no goodt. I'dt be wastin' both our time."

"Be glad to. *Proper names of people, places, and things begin wite a capital letter, such as Roy, Muskogee Library, and Laubach Literacy Program.*" He turned, waiting.

"Great. Now, let's look back at this word right here," I said, holding my hand under *wite*. He slowly read it again, both to himself and out loud, glancing from each word on my original long card to the actual words he had printed so meticulously.

"*Proper names of people, places, and things begin wite. . . .* With! Yep, I got that wrong. It shouldt be WITH." He shook his head and corrected his paper, chiding himself the whole time. "I shoulda seen that."

"Well, let's look at this another way. You found your own mistake. I did not point it out to you. And you have written all the other words and punctuation marks on this long card correctly, which was more than I could do the first time! You only missed one word, and only by one letter. You did great."

"Trude, there's one thing you gotta understandt here 'bout this copyin' a mine. I can-not git it all at onc'dt. I gots'ta go in bits 'n pieces, letter by letter on the writin' a them wordts. That makes it real slow, 'n real tirin'. My handt cramps up.

"All a this is still so new 'ta me that it makes me nervous. I'm so afear'dt that I'll make me a mistake, that I cain't hardt-ly con-centrate on learnin' how'ta spell them wordts right now. I guess what I'm tryin'ta tell ya is, that I'm still in the baby steps. But I'm a goin' forwardt. That's the only'est part that counts."

It was here that I told Roy about ancient Monks and their laborious copying of Bibles and priceless manuscripts in the early centuries. By candlelight, by hand — and in ink!

"After hours of work, these men could be at the bottom of a page, and then make one simple mistake. Poof! Their efforts would go out the window. At least you have a pencil with an eraser, Roy. You do not have to write in ink. Monks did not have that luxury.

"Just remember, before you are too hard on yourself, that you are in good company. Others have traveled the road of copying. You are not alone. Monks did good. You do good. Those manuscripts of theirs that survive to this day are very, very valuable. Your efforts are valuable, too. Stay focused on that." He smiled.

Innocuously, I asked what seemed to be a simple question. I should have known better.

"Mr. Caddell, do you realize how far you have come in only seven short days? In only seven class meetings?"

"I think I do. . . ." He paused to reflect. "But, maybe not." Extemporaneously, I listed what we had accomplished. Together.

"You have learned the entire alphabet, and that there are only twenty-six letters in the dern thing. You have read and learned the words they have given us to this point, and can comfortably read and recognize most on sight.

"You have learned to form your mouth in unfamiliar ways in order to make some very difficult sounds, like PARAGRAPH.

"You have learned about apostrophe -S, and that it is used to denote ownership.

"You have learned that every sentence begins with a capital letter and ends with some form of punctuation, and basically, you have learned what those marks are. You know that proper names of people, places and things begin with capital letters.

"You have learned that book titles are underlined; and that newspaper and magazine titles usually are written in quotation marks. You have learned it is best to read with expression in your voice.

"You have learned the seven vowels, and that every word has at least one vowel in it. You are learning those extremely difficult short vowel sounds, although this one might take us years!

"You have learned that the letter Q is always followed by the letter U. You have learned about paragraphs and their importance.

"You have learned to print and write in cursive all of your letters so that you and others can read what you have written. You pass. I flunk." Roy laughed. I cried.

"You have learned about syllables and how they make big words easier to break down, sound out and, hopefully, then spell.

"You have started using a dictionary to look up words so that you can check your spellings and see what those words mean. I have learned your wish is that I would put the dern thing away, permanently! Good luck on this one, Friend!" We both laughed.

"You have learned of word endings, which change the way in which a word may be used. You have heard me refer several times to singular and plural, and at least know of what I am speaking.

"You have learned to look for tiny Words Within Words, to help you spell and perhaps even sound out a word for yourself. You have learned to spell a number of words in their entirety, and can readily tell me what letter almost any word I give you begins with.

"You have learned that you can change one letter in a word, a vowel, to make another new word with an entirely different meaning.

"You have learned each letter has its own distinct sound, and many letters work together to make different sounds when combined, such as -SH, -CH and -TH, your favorite." I grinned. He did not.

"You have learned about daily newspapers, and where to find information in them. You have learned that most of our world operates on the Printed Word.

"You have learned about pyramids and logical progressions, and I have learned that you like them both.

"You have read your first book, but not your last! YIPPEE!

"And, you have learned that coming here to do this Education Business, among virtual strangers, is not such a horrid thing. There are some really nice people in this world who truly want to help you." It was my turn to grin sheepishly.

He sat there shaking his head in awe and disbelief, at exactly what he had been exposed to and accomplished, in an unbelievably short time. He was stunned. A joyous smile warmed his well-lined face. At that moment, Roy Caddell looked like a younger man. Finally, he spoke.

"I never knowt there was that much 'ta all a this. I haf learnt me a bunch, Trude. I haf. But, what I can-not figur' out, is why I like it so much. Even the parts I hate!"

The distance traveled by this one man in seven short days was monumental, off the charts. I was in awe of him and his dogged tenacity. He made my spirits soar.

As we walked out of the library that day, we chatted about the weekend driving trip he and his wife were taking to visit relatives in Arkansas. I could tell Roy was excited.

"But now, don't forgit. My wife shore is lookin' forward'ta comin' here w'th me on Monday." Of course, I had not forgotten.

"But," I interjected, suddenly realizing I had never asked the question, "you have got to tell me her name! I cannot simply call her 'wife.'"

"Hazel," he warmly responded in smiles. "She's a might-y nice person." We were at our cars and I turned to give him a hug.

"Have a wonderful time and be careful. I love you and I shall see you both on Monday." I thought of them often that weekend and wished them well from afar.

HAZEL AND WORDS

"I don't knowt if I can r'member nuthin' today, I'm
jist so nervous. I guess'dt it's 'cause she's sittin' here.
We been over 'n over all them wordts at home, 'n I
knowt 'em this mornin' befor' we start'dt out. But, I
shore don't knowt 'bout now."

Honk! Honk! My now familiar greeting filled the air as I rounded the corner in excited anticipation. "You knew I would be here," I exclaimed as I bounded from my car.

"I toldt my wife we'd knowt when it'ud be straight up nine o'clock, 'cause you'd be roundin' that corner," he said laughingly as he walked towards me, a big smile on his face.

"He told me you always honk," she chuckled softly, descending from a shiny blue truck. I liked her immediately.

"Hazel, I'm Trude Norman," I said extending my hand. "I'm so glad you could come today! Thank you."

"Well. I'm Hazel," she replied, meeting my hand warmly. "I sure have heard a lot about you and I've really been looking forward to meeting you. He talks about you all the time."

"He's not the only one! My family and friends think your husband has become a part of our immediate world. I refer to him all the time as *my little reading man.*" She grinned. We chatted easily as we walked to the library, Roy saying nothing. Just walking proud.

Upstairs the three of us visited a long while at the conference table, with Hazel choosing to sit across from Roy and me. It was obvious she wanted this Education Business to work for her husband. I liked that. In my family, the men and women are supportive of one another. Hazel Caddell was Roy's underpinning.

"Weren't you the one who originally called the Muskogee Public Library, Hazel, to see if there were a literacy program?"

The National Literacy number is 1-800-228-8813, but you will not find it in a phone book. Nor will you find an 800 number for literacy programs within a state. This is a travesty. Nonreaders needing help to learn how to read and write do not know where to go for tutoring. That is wrong. We as a nation are doing a horrid job publicizing one of the most vital places where nearly 50 percent of our adult population can turn to improve their reading skills.

"Yes. I tried several other places first — it was not easy to find where to call — and then finally, I called here. They were very nice and referred me to the lady, whom I believe contacted you."

That was Delia Brown. How lucky the literacy program was to have her. She was dynamite at her job, particularly adept at making people feel comfortable. She was even, steady and highly intelligent. Roy liked her.

"Hazel, I must tell you that I have heard the nicest things about you. I want you to know how very, very much I appreciate all you have done to help your husband, and me. You have made my job easier by supporting our many and varied endeavors. Thank you." She smiled. Roy had told me of her repeated efforts with homework, which kept his learning at the forefront on days he was not in school.

"I've tried to help, and I do," she responded. "I told him that this was his responsibility, but that I will do everything I can to help." She looked his way softly and added, "He loves coming to school. Thank you for helping him."

"You two are em-barrassin' me. I think I better learn'ta keep my mouth shut more." We all laughed.

"OK, Friend, let's see what you have been working on." His face suddenly took on an ashen pallor as he realized casual conversation was over. Anxiously, he pulled out his things. We were down to "brass tacks."

"I don't knowt if I can r'member nuthin' today, I'm jist so nervous. I guess'dt it's 'cause she's sittin' here. We been over 'n over all them wordts at home, 'n I knowt 'em this mornin' befor' we start'dt out. But," he said shaking his head uncertainly, "I shore don't knowt 'bout now."

"Yes, you do," I gently urged, looking him straight in the eye. "You *know* these words. I have absolute confidence in you. We are going to take this slowly and we will both do fine." He did not return my smile.

The previous lesson I had asked Roy to concentrate on his printing. Initially, his writing was erratic. He combined capital and small letters in the same word. Such obviously primitive factors would give him away. This was to be avoided at all costs. Practice would be his ticket to security and freedom.

We had covered parts of this earlier, but not in depth. I knew bad habits set into motion would stay with him the rest of his life — and be nearly impossible to correct, if not caught now.

First, we covered the words he had written at home on his own. He had done much work in preparation for today, and had done a fine job. I told him so, and he noticeably relaxed.

"He's been practicing," Hazel said, watching us intently. That he had, but there was more.

On several pages of his yellow legal tablet, he had written out all of the words he had been given to date. He had made two long columns.

Along the left margin, he had printed each word on separate lines going down the page, one right after another. On the right side of the paper he had written, *in cursive,* all these same words again. Both the printed and cursive versions of each word were written on the same line, opposite one another. Again, he had done a beautiful job.

This had to have been a slow, arduous task. Even simple copying is tedious and tiring. Like our monks, Roy had spent long hours preparing for this lesson his wife was to attend.

His mistakes were easy to correct, nothing major. He had merely transposed letters in many of the words. It was easy to see which words needed correcting and which did not, because not all did. Some were printed incorrectly in the left column, yet written correctly in cursive in the second column. Some were the opposite.

I held my hand under the first misspelled word and gently asked, "Please read to me what you printed here and then what you wrote in cursive over here."

"I jist cain't seem'ta do nuthin' today."

"Quite the contrary. You have done quite well. I did not ask you to write any of these words in that *fancy writin'* stuff you mentioned on Day One. You did this by yourself, and did a fine job.

"You have all the letters right for every word. Some of the letters are merely turned around. That's all. Everyone transposes letters. Or, at least," I laughed, "every journalist I know does." He realized my intent and finally smiled.

"You meant, I've jist writ-ten sum'a them wordts back'ards?"

"Exactly. The rest is great. But, you said that far better than I. Backwards is the perfect word to use here, I simply did not think of it." He beamed and looked relieved.

"Boy howdy. F'r a minute there, I thought I was in trouble."

Hazel was sitting silently as we worked, she scarcely moved. She made no attempt to enter into our lesson. Wisely, she had chosen not to correct her husband's homework. Roy would not be unhappy with me when I did, he was used to that. But today, he might have been with her. Because if ever Roy Caddell wanted to have his homework right, this would have been the day.

I had but one innocuous game plan on schedule for today, which I was about to throw out to Mr. Caddell. It was a curve ball he was not expecting, but a ball he could easily catch. I had no intention of starting new work this day. There were too many areas we could review and still cover new ground. This was one.

"Roy, I have brought words printed on cards. I have mixed them up so they are not in any particular order. Otherwise, you would recognize them quickly and say them back to me from memory.

"They are all words you have read to me before. I want you to read them again to me please. I want to show you something."

I deliberately said these "are all words you have read to me before." I did not say these "are all words you *know!*" Major difference. His attention piqued, although he looked a bit puzzled. We were at the heart of the lesson and he was sitting up straight in his chair, glasses on, ready to work.

The first word card I held up was LOOKED. He promptly read it correctly. I think NAMED was next and, though he faltered ever so slightly, he got it. Then, I presented SUDDENLY. He knew that, too. He was pleased, and so was I. FLUTTERED came next and he stumbled, making a guess.

"Feathered?" he queried. Quickly he became deflated.

To have embarrassed Roy Caddell in front of his wife would have been horribly cruel. Unthinkable. He would have felt not only mortified, but he could have lost heart entirely. Such was never my intention.

I had made up my mind in preparing this lesson, that I would let him truly miss only one word before I let him in on the game plan for the day. My whole purpose was for him to read something in front of Hazel that he had read before to me, and to himself. Something he *knew* he could read, Walt Disney's short story.

At the same time, I wanted the three of us to be aware that just because he could read words together in a story, did not mean he *knew* every word on a given page. He did not.

Thus, I did not have Roy first read a page from *The Fox and the Hound* and then go over each word separately. I did the exact opposite, which gave us entirely new learning opportunities.

Mine was the Back Door Approach. Once again, it might not have been *the* best. It only seemed best for us.

Stories are words. To read means to recognize and comprehend the same words over and over and over. Reading words once does not constitute knowing words, as he had just demonstrated.

Roy Caddell could certainly read that Disney page to me, but I did not remotely think he *knew* every word on that page, if each word were shown separately to him. He did not. He was not aware of this pervasive fact until now. My bottom line was for Roy to look and feel good in front of his wife today, while still covering new ground. It worked.

"I want to show you something, Roy, and I want you to read it to me." I pulled out the tiny booklet he had read five days earlier, which I had casually "borrowed" without explaining why. He broke into smiles and immediately perked up. *Now* he knew where we were going. This was familiar territory, comfortable terrain. His body noticeably relaxed as he went to work.

> *"One sunny morning," he confidently began to read, "Big Mama the owl looked down from her perch high above the forest. Suddenly, something caught her eye. It was a little ball of bright red fur hiding in the tall grass below. She fluttered down to take a closer look. 'Well fuss my feathers! A baby fox all alone in this world!' worried Big Mama. But Big Mama knew a kind lady, named Widow Tweed, who would love the dear little fox."*

End of page one. He had stumbled only once. He looked over at me, grinning. He knew now he could do this work today and not embarrass himself.

"Always move from the known to the unknown" is the Laubach theory. It gives a student a feeling of confidence and progress. We followed this guide to the letter. I but rearranged the rules.

"Now, Roy, please count the number of words on this one page that you just read. I want you to see something."

"One, two, three . . . seventy-five, seventy-six. I count seventy-six. That's alotta wordts now," he exclaimed in amazement.

"I agree. But, before we read this story, you did not realize that you knew that many different words. Some of them are hard words, Roy. You knew most the first time we read this story. You know them now. You read this page beautifully both times.

"But, I had a hunch that what you could *read* in a story, and then recognize on sight and *know* every single time, were two vastly different creatures." His eyes were riveted to mine. He sat like a statue.

"I merely want us to be aware that, just because we can read words in story form, does *not* necessarily mean we actually *know* every word in that story. We might not.

"I read words in books. Most I know. Some, I do not. I figure out the meaning of some words by their context, the way they are used in a sentence. *But,* that still does not mean I know every word. I do not.

"That is why I constantly use a dictionary. Why I must hear and see a word over and over again before it becomes a part of my vocabulary. You are no different from anyone else in that respect. Be good to yourself. That's what I want you to remember." He grinned warmly, and we finished rereading our marvelous Disney tale.

Still, Hazel scarcely moved. I had no idea what she thought of our lesson or our disjointed conversations. I never asked. We both had all but forgotten she was there.

For us, this was routine, normal; and yet, to an outsider, absolutely abnormal. What a strange and roundabout method we had of getting in the front door. What a strange pair we must have been. Only a small part of every lesson was spent teaching "by the book." The rest was expended in learning through philosophical discussions. We covered the waterfront, the world.

But, Roy said it best: "I like the talkin' part as well as the learnin' part. 'N I never thought I wouldt."

The last exercise we did before leaving on that eighth day was to draw up a list of words important to Roy Caddell — words from his world. He had mentioned this any number of times, and again today. Remembering his comments, I waited until Hazel's visit to draw up such a list. I wanted her input and help. I wanted to include her in our day.

So, the three of us sat and tossed out words across the table from one another until we could think of no more. The two of them did the thinking. I did the writing . . . poor choice! They could barely read my list.

Our words were TRACTOR, HAY BALER, CALF, BRUSH HOG, TILLER, SALE, GARDEN, SHREDDER, PLOW, COW, DOG, HAT, FENCE, POST HOLE DIGGER, PICKUP, MOWER, GRINDER, TRUCK, TRAILER, BARN, HOUSE, SOW, PLOW, HAUL, SEED, TOOLS, TREES, POND, BALE, FEED, FIELD, PASTURE, FISH, STACK, MOVE and TANK.

We would add more as we thought of them, but for now, this was a great start. I would go home and make cards for each. Soon we would be off in another new direction of learning, and of challenge. Perhaps, we would never be finished. Perhaps no one ever is.

It had been a good lesson. I was thrilled Hazel had come, as was Roy. We left the library relaxed and laughing, feeling positive about our day together. We were visiting as we walked to our cars, Roy between the two of us, when he quietly said something that floored me. I was speechless.

"I toldt Hazel 'bout how last time you toldt me you loved me. That was mighty nice a you."

"Yes, he did," Hazel immediately added, dead serious. "That really made an impression on him. He came home and told me what you had said to him."

Never would I have thought shy, quiet Roy Caddell would have mentioned this again to me. I vividly remember he was taken aback when I said it. But the words, which I say often to people I care about, were out of my mouth before I could catch them. He must have sensed this. My only thought at the time was that I hoped I had not embarrassed him. Obviously not.

As I climbed into my car, Roy tipped his hat and softly said, "Love ya, too."

It had indeed been a very good day! This time, *I* floated home.

DICTION ON PAPER

*"It's like I was tellin' my wife this mornin' befor' she
left. As nice as you 'n Trude both are, and as much as I
know you try 'n understandt what it's like f'r me not
'ta haf an ed-ucashun, you jist cain't. You both cain't
never know what it's real-ly like not 'ta be able'ta readt
'n write. You cain't know. . . ."*

Even before I was out of my car the next day we met, Roy was talking.
Spring was in full bloom and my window was down. I heard him as he
stood by the curb beside a shade tree, which puzzled me. I had never
seen him anywhere but beside his truck. He did not budge, so I headed
his way. He stopped only long enough for greeting. Then he started
again.

"Singles? Isn't that what that word there says? Singles?" I nodded
my head as it hit me like a ton of bricks. This man had been "studyin'"
the only word he did not know on a sign across the street.

"I been figurin' on it awhile now, 'n I was pret-ty shore it really was
that. But, I had'ta knowt f'r certain." His white hat was cocked on his
head and his eyes twinkling as we headed to the library. Now he knew
he *could* read something in the real world beyond our classroom.

"Now, this here is what I done at home f'r you to check," Roy offered
when asked about homework. "I didn't real-ly get too much done," he
inferred, turning in his yellow legal tablet to where he had written the
lower case letters of the alphabet. Twenty-six full lines on that page were
covered with the most beautiful writing I had seen in a very long time.
I was stunned.

"Roy! This is positively beautiful. These letters are all perfectly
formed and written legibly, every one of them. Anyone could read these.
Why, most college-educated people cannot write this well. Almost no
one can read a doctor's handwriting and signature, or even a lawyer's.

"Almost no one can read mine. You have worked and worked on these letters, Mr. Caddell. It shows, I am impressed!" He positively glowed.

"Well now, Trude. Me 'n Hazel was talkin' this mornin' 'bout that very thing. You *do* needt help w'th y'ur writin'. Hazel done toldt you she'd be glad 'ta help you anytime y'ur ready, she writes real goodt. Maybe soon *I'll* make you up a sheet a them letters 'ta practice on. . . ." His eyes twinkled mischievously.

"You know I flunk there," I laughed. "The bad news is that my handwriting still leaves much to be desired. The good news is that my spelling most definitely has improved with our dictionary usage in class. At least, I am now batting 50/50."

The day Hazel was with us, she was silently aghast at my penmanship. I saw it in her face. There I was trying to show her husband how to write, yet neither could read what I wrote. There were twists and swirls and embellishments such that few — my mother and my children, can read what I write. It's bad.

Little did Roy know that I *had* been practicing, with every note I wrote, every list I made. He had made gigantic strides in this department. I had not. One of us had to write so the other could read it. He was the designated hitter. I was the water boy. Years later, our roles have not reversed.

At this point in time, we added another new dimension to our lessons: directed silent reading. There was no advance warning. Just one day, it was there. Boom!

In directed silent reading, students read the day's story silently to themselves and *then* answer the teacher's questions out loud. After today's lesson, Roy never again read the assigned story aloud to me. This was an abrupt change for my friend. It initially threw him and made him anxious.

"'Ta be able 'ta readt 'n understandt this ed-ucashun stuff, I gotta follow the rules. Those wordts look stupid 'ta me. Ever' time I stumble 'n wrench my knee on this stuff ya wouldn't let me skip over, I knowt I'm gonna be gladt."

"Boy now. I don't know as I'm gonna like this. . . ."

The intent of directed silent reading was multi-faceted: It encouraged Roy in his reading comprehension and verbalization skills, by testing his knowledge *out loud* for us both to hear.

The concept gave him confidence in his own capabilities, by forcing him to verbalize what he had just read. It also forced him to listen to the sound of his voice as he expressed himself and carefully enunciated words. Both were vital.

Verbalization and listening skills are always terribly lacking for one such as Roy. When people who cannot read begin to learn, they are initially shocked that *they can actually be reading* anything out loud to anyone. Roy was no exception. His own reading voice scared him.

Our story words for Lessons Six through Nine had been selected to demonstrate the use of capital letters with proper names of people and places. According to Laubach directions, we were to go through the alphabet in sequential order, omitting only the letters X and Z. We had been working on capitalizing for some time now, as exemplified by our long punctuation card. Roy was warming up to the concept.

Lesson Seven's workbook assignment targeted another critical area, one I had not covered. The lesson focus was two-fold:

One. Simple words that, when capitalized, give needed identification as to location or title: INDIAN VALLEY, QUEEN.

Two. Double consonants working together in a person's name that make but one sound: ANN, JILL, HILL, GLENN and CADDELL.

With every lesson story, there were simple questions I asked of Roy. Each was important. Each reinforced the intent of directed silent reading. I could quickly ascertain if we were headed in the right direction or down the wrong path. We could not afford a slip. Each building block to that pyramid had to be solidly in place.

"How many people are in the Hill family, Roy?"

"Ahhh. Four."

"Where do they live?"

"Ummm. Valley?"

"Well. They actually live in *Indian* Valley. See how both words are capitalized in the sentence and in the title of the story up there?" I said pointing to darker words at the top of the lesson page.

"Ahhh. Oh, yeah. Now I see it."

"Who is kicking the ball and who is catching it in this story?"

"Well, let's see now . . . Jill? Jill is kickin' the ball, 'n that there other one is a catchin' it?"

"Not quite. Let's look back here and read that again. Then see what you think..."

"Oh, yeah. Kim is kickin' the ball, 'n Jill there is jumpin'ta catch it. I see that now."

"Roy. I do not want you to look at the pictures and guess. I want you to read the words, by first concentrating on the letters and then sounding them out. Back to Square One. I want you to be certain of what you have read. This is not a guessing game."

Slowly, over many sessions, he could answer my questions as to exactly what he just read in any given lesson story. But it was not easy. When I asked him to point out to me why he gave a particular response, he would run his finger down the page to find the exact paragraph and place in the story where it was so stated. This, I told him, is called "scanning," which simply means, to rapidly go over great quantities of materials to find specific facts.

"Some people call it 'perusing.' Either way, you often will find yourself doing this to find answers. Eventually, scanning becomes everyone's friend, Roy. It is a helpful tool in reading. I use it all the time. You will like it, too." He smiled.

In our lesson on vowels, I had told Roy that "the word AN must be used before any singular word, or noun beginning with a vowel. No exceptions. *This* one you must memorize." Which he did, and rarely missed thereafter.

Today, I printed four words on his yellow legal tablet I knew he would detest: AN, AND, ANN and ANNE. AND he had encountered a few lessons earlier, but it plagued him still. ANN was the Laubach workbook example.

"If ya see all them letters 'n wordts in strange places, they don't mean nuthin' when ya cain't readt 'n write. We don't knowt if they're in the right place 'r not. All we knowt is that each a them is im-port'nt. The two ANNs are that way f'r me."

My feeling was that "you can't have one ANN without the other." Roy's eyes opened wide as I finished writing all four. He turned to me, befuddled. He had no idea what I was showing him.

When Roy Caddell first began our classes, he had absolutely no concept of the word AND. He could not pronounce it. He could not read it. He could not spell it. He simply shrugged his shoulders.

Even the base word A, he had been unsure of initially. We had gone over it as to meaning, usage and intent. We were making slow progress.

For Roy however, the conjunction AND was another matter. It was written "A" or "AN," which required another explanation and more discussion. To this day, he tends to pronounce AND as AN. I *make* him enunciate the "d" on the end. He'd just as soon leave it off.

So, for us to finally get to ANN in our lessons, we had gone over the mountain and down in the valley several times. Down we went again. As I finished writing ANN and ANNE, I turned to look at him and pointedly asked, "Please read these words to me."

"Trude, I ain't got no i-dear. I knowt y'ur tryin'ta tell me somethin' real im-port'nt, but it's not takin' yet. Y'ur tellin' me that all four a them wordts is pronounc'dt close 'ta the same ways, but don't any a them mean the same thing? Why wouldt they try 'n trick us like that?" So . . . once again, we began. Finally, it took.

"What y'ur a tellin' me here is that them first two ANNs you couldt write in little letters; but them other two, you couldt never write that way. It'ud al-ways haf'ta be in big letters." Brilliant! My mouth flew open before I dissolved into laughter.

"Well. Ya gotta knowt when 'ta use proper respect w'th y'ur pencil. Isn't that what this is? Ya capit-tilize 'ta show respect, even I know that. It shore makes sense't here. Nuthin' els'dt much does.

"One thing 'bout it, Trude. I did not readt it somewheres. Maybe I will somedays. . . ." He leaned back in his chair, grinning at the dead aim he had taken on these four small words.

Still laughing, I shrugged my shoulders and closed his tablet. End of lesson. He had scored a bulls-eye with one shot.

Then, off we took on another tangent and another logical progression. This, I thought, would be fun.

As I had looked at the simple lesson words JILL and HILL, my immediate thought was that if we changed the first letter of each, we would have an entirely new learning opportunity. To me, this was one of the greatest things we ever did in the first workbook. We still do it, five years later. I call it Word Volley, or Diction on Paper. It was as if the word JILL dictated new words.

Mentally, I tried each letter of the alphabet that would make an actual word out of JILL. Then, I called these "new" words out to him.

"OK, Roy. Please open your tablet again and listen before you write one thing. What new word would you have if you changed the first letter of JILL, the J, to a B? I want you to picture this word in your head, to *see* it in your mind's eye, before you write even one letter. What would the word B-I-L-L spell?"

He caught on quickly as he "studied" the words in thin air each time before applying pencil to paper. It was fun to *watch* his mind at work.

Thus, JILL quickly became BILL, DILL, FILL, GILL, HILL, ILL, KILL, MILL, PILL, QUILL, RILL, SILL, TILL and WILL. With each word, Roy added yet another new word to his ever increasing vocabulary.

As he honed these new skills, I pointedly reversed the plan of attack. No writing this time around. This was mental gymnastics.

First, I would spell the very words out loud to him that he had written on his tablet, then ask, "What word are we now spelling? No looking back to see what you have just written."

Each time, I urged him to see the word in his mind's eye. It did not take him long to become a tactician here as well.

"What would you have if the word were spelled M-I-L-L?"

"Ahhh. Mill?"

"Yes. What if it were spelled S-I-L-L?"

"Ummm. Sill?"

"Exactly. T-I-L-L?"

"Ahhh. Till?"

"Right again!"

It became a volley of words, my questions and his answers. Rat-a-tat-tat. He took to these drills like a duck to water. Our Word Volley became a game with a purpose, a game I played with a vengeance, and a smile. I never forgot that our bottom line was to teach this one man to read and write.

These simple words soon became stamped on Roy's brain as to spelling, meaning, pronunciation, recognition. All were new to him. All were different. All absolutely fascinated this man.

Countless workbook words over the years became launching pads from which we took off on yet other tangents and drills. Simple words were logical progressions I could not skirt.

Eventually, BILL became BUILD, then BUILT; DILL became DRILL and DRUM; KILL led to KILT and KING; PILL to PULL and PUSH; SILL to STILL and WILL to WELL. WELL he detested for years. WILL would have covered the waterfront.

To me, this was first-class learning. This was the essence of a liberal education. He deserved no less.

As we were leaving that day, Roy Caddell suddenly knocked me into the middle of next week with a commentary that brought me close to tears. His quick mind shifted gears with startling clarity.

"It's like I was tellin' my wife this mornin' befor' she left. As nice as you 'n Trude both are, and as much as I knowt you try 'n understandt what it's like f'r me not 'ta haf an ed-ucashun, you jist cain't. You both cain't never knowt what it's *real-ly* like not 'ta be able'ta readt 'n write. You cain't know." He shook his head and looked dead ahead. There was no smile. He never glanced my way.

He had been in some low lonely valleys. I swallowed hard and felt my heart crack. I was not expecting this. I kept my own eyes dead ahead until I found my voice. He deserved a response.

"No, Roy. You are right. I cannot possibly know what it is like not to have an education. Or how complex all this learning must be from your perspective. I am truly sorry."

"No. You cain't. Neither can Hazel. Trude, I knowt I'll never be at y'ur level. No ways. But, that's OK. I'm learnin'. And I'm *real* gladt I come here to do this. Thank you f'r bein' the one 'ta help me." He turned my way and smiled his gratitude. I could only smile back and hope he would keep talking.

Never, in my wildest dreams, did I think I would be walking beside a friend and hear such words come out of his mouth. It was beyond comprehension. I can still *hear* Roy Caddell walking from that library and looking down at that pavement, as he peeled yet another layer of protective coating, another layer of shame.

My face was flushed by the hot sun and his simplistic words. He knew how to cut to the chase. He was one heckuva teacher himself.

THE ROCKY ROAD OF SHAME

*Three-hundred words are a mere drop in the bucket. No
one writes anything of substance with a three-hundred
word vocabulary. No one reads a newspaper with a
three-hundred word vocabulary. No one reads a book of
any consequence with a three-hundred word
vocabulary. No one operates well in the literate world
with a three-hundred word vocabulary.*

At our Friday lesson before Memorial Day weekend, I pulled up beside
Roy's truck and leaned out the window. "Remember all those words
you and Hazel and I came up with together?"

"Ahhh. Yep."

"Well. Have I got a surprise for you!"

"You brung me them wordts!" He could scarcely contain his excitement, waiting to get upstairs.

"First, though, let's walk this way. I want to show you something."

As I wheeled around the corner only moments before, I had noticed that
the tall marquee outside the library read, "Walk Softly and Carry a Big
Book." Having recently finished Edith and Alice, the story of Teddy
Roosevelt's two wonderful but very different wives, I loved the sign.

The parking lot was virtually deserted, only two empty cars. I took
care to stand behind the corner of the building, blocking the front door
from sight. No one would hear me ask him to read, nor would they
guess why we were standing beneath the marquee, looking up.

"Can you read this to me?" I gently asked.

"Ahhh. Yes. It says, 'Walk Softly and Carry a Big Book.'"

"Do you know what the original statement was and who made it?"
He did not miss a beat, his reply was quick and confident.

"Teddy Roosevelt. He said, 'Walk softly and carry a big stick.'" I let
out a tiny yell of joy. He grinned.

"Trude, there ain't no tellin' what I'da done w'th my life if I'da had me an ed-ucashun. Ain't no tellin' how smart I'da been."

In this man's mind, Education = Smart. No Education = Dumb. Inconceivable. He had no idea how smart and capable he truly was.

As we turned to the not-yet-open library, there were already three people waiting, at nine o'clock in the morning. I had no idea America's public libraries were so busy. They are, every single day.

When we were settled upstairs at the conference table, I pulled out a posterboard with his words printed down its length, one right after the other. I used one big card because I wanted Roy to see the words as a group, as he remembered them. Individual cards I would make and bring later. He happily took the offered list.

"Now, Friend. Please read these to me."

Some he could read, some he could not. Some he could decipher only by guessing, because they were double or triple words that he could recognize by their numbers, like HAY BALER or POST HOLE DIGGER.

Others, like HAT and FENCE, stumped him. Especially HAT, he could not read that tiny word. He was dejected. I was dumbfounded. This man wore a hat every single day of his life! It was an integral part of who he was. Yet, he could not read the word. He could not spell it.

We had our work cut out for us. Once again, we began.

We commenced dissecting his words, slowly tearing them apart. I asked him the sounds and letters that began each. We sounded out every one. When I placed my hand over the H in HAT so he could see the familiar and tiny word AT, he immediately responded, thoroughly disgusted with himself, "A cours't. Now, I shoulda seen that."

No. He should have *sounded* it out. He had the tools to read these words. He had to will his mind to use them. It was hard.

Next we looked for Words Within Words, always challenging. He especially liked doing that for TRACTOR.

"Why, I never knowt there was that many wordts insid'a TRACTOR. And sum'a them are little." (ACT, ACTOR, OR, TRACT, TACT) Then I told him if we changed the letter C to I, we would have the word TRAITOR. His eyebrows went up. He saw that clearly, now.

For precaution, we went back over the entire word card again quickly, reading down the length and then back up. He did a nice job. He knew each word in the order I had written them, in the order he had repeated them. Now I wanted to see if he knew them out of order.

Randomly, I pointed to various words, skipping around the card in no particular sequence. Most he read correctly and without hesitation. He perked up. He *did* know these words, today. Tomorrow might be another story.

Several weeks later I brought Roy's Words back on individual cards, which tickled him. As we reviewed each, he scarcely missed a one. He had added another forty words to his ever-growing repertoire.

These words were important *for* Roy Caddell because they were important *to* Roy Caddell. They were tangible words, from his world. They also represented encouragement. He needed all he could get if he were to stay in this competitive game.

His handicap here was that he had to both learn and unlearn. He had to forget what had brought him to this point, in order now to absorb what would carry him forward. It was an ongoing struggle. I often wondered if he felt he were a vise being turned on itself. Painful.

Random Word Check, my terminology, is the helpful practice of drilling students on words that are presented to them, *in no meaningful order.* It is absolutely crucial in teaching nonreaders, whose primary tool is memory. I did not know this, nor even suspect it, until Roy told me.

"Trude, it ain't the things we don't know that causes us trouble. It's the things we do know. I got too much 'ta forget first." I was astounded. What this boiled down to was that Roy Caddell's past memory was hindering his present learning.

"THAT MIXIN' UP THEM WORDTS WAS ONE A THE BEST THINGS YA COULDT'A DONE F'R MY ED-UCASHUN. I AL-WAYS TRIED'TA MEMORIZE WHAT WORDTS I COULDT, 'CAUSE FA-MILIAR'TY WAS HOW I GOT BY — HOW I LIV'DT. BUT YOU MADE'T IT MORE OF A CHALLENGE ON ME, 'N I NEED'DT THAT."

Memory to me meant mastering and remembering data correctly. Memory to nonreaders meant survival.

They have honed their memories razor sharp over long years of coping, getting by. They rely totally on what they have heard or overheard; on what they have seen; on what they have been told; on what they have been shown; on what has been read to them; or on what they have tried to read to themselves. Correctly, or incorrectly.

Memory is great for short term, but it is a poor substitute for the long run — and no substitute for actual reading skills. Huge difference. For me, this was Basic Indoctrination #101.

Roy Caddell had conditioned himself mentally over long years to *believe* he could not know a word, thus, he could not read a word. He had rendered himself immobile, suspended in a time warp.

His first instinct, and often his first answer, was *guess!* Such total lack of self confidence and inbred hostility toward basic education and learning hindered every step we took through the first workbook. It does not make our work easy, even today.

This morning, I had brought a flier from the National Literacy Council inviting students and teachers to write on the topic, "How Learning to Read Opened My World." I was interested, but I wanted Roy's feelings. If he were willing, we would do this. If not, we would not. I would not turn in anything without his participation.

This was not a casual thing to this man. I almost could hear his brain churning. This one-page leaflet represented potential danger and exposure. Whatever action we took, would have to be solely his decision.

"You meant," he finally said, staring at the paper which he, too, had received — but trashed — "that I'd write somethin' 'bout how I like all this and how it's help'dt me?" I nodded.

"Couldt I," he slowly quizzed, "tell my wife what I wanna say, 'n then she couldt write it down f'r me?"

"Yes. But, let me check to be positive. What Hazel writes would have to be your exact words. Then you would have to copy those words in your own handwriting to turn in for publication. They want your words and feelings, Roy, not mine or Hazel's." His meditation continued.

"Then, I think I'd like'ta do this, Trude. I think it wouldt help me. I'm willin'ta do anythin' that'll help me. Or you. But, I shore couldn't tell ever'thing I want'dta on just one page." Nor could I, Mr. Caddell. Nor could I.

Casually, I asked Roy if he would like to see the first page of the book I was writing about our experience together — that I would turn in for publication, were he agreeable.

He slowly shook his head in disbelief as he gingerly reached for my opening page. He had heard me speak of this project before, as I always kept him abreast of progress. But until that moment, I do not think Roy Caddell remotely thought such writing might become reality.

"I *cannot* i-magine what it is y'ur a writin' 'bout me," he very tentatively responded. "I wanna read it, no matter what it says. But, I cain't hardt-ly believe y'ur doin' this f'r me." He kept shaking his head as he gently held the paper, looking it up and down as if it might speak to him.

"That is exactly why I am doing this, Roy. For you. It is my gift to you, with love." Then haltingly I asked, not knowing how else to broach the subject, "Would you like for me to read it to you?"

"Yes. I shore wouldt." His eyes shone.

There was a wondrous look on his face as he gingerly offered the paper back to me. I still can see that man sitting there, *watching* that paper held in his rough hands, wishing so the page would open up to reveal its content.

Slowly I began, observing him out of the corner of my eye as I read. He never looked from the page. He never moved a muscle. He was so still by the time I finished, I hoped I had not offended him.

Finally, he turned quietly and said, "You done goodt here, Trude. Real goodt. This must be some book y'ur writin' if the rest of it soundts like this. This soundts like somethin' you couldt go to the store 'n buy.

"Only, Trude," he sheepishly paused. "I ain't never been in no *bookstore* befor'." My hand flew to my mouth, I literally was taken aback. He kept shaking his head, as if any minute now he might awaken from this fantasy. *Someone writing about him?* Impossible dream.

What I had not previously understood about individuals such as Roy, is that they seldom ask questions of anyone, i.e., his asking me to read that one page to him. He never would have asked. Too often, nonreaders will sadly do without before they ask for help. They will cheat themselves before they risk embarrassing themselves. They are caught on a high suspension bridge, and it's a long way down.

Oftentimes, if others — particularly close family members — see a dilemma and offer help, nonreaders become angry, defensive, offended and ultimately, defeated. There is no winning here, only losing.

Here are responsible people who are bright, intelligent, capable, contributing members of society. They work hard at jobs, have families, pay taxes. Yet, they are unwilling to ask for help.

Roy Caddell *never* would have come right out and asked me to read that first page of my manuscript to him. It saddened me.

We were moving right along with the capital letters of the alphabet, used when denoting specific titles or names. Lesson Eight's workbook examples were MR. and MRS. I threw in MISS and MS. If Roy had heard of one of them, he had *heard* of all of them — he batted 100 percent, four out of four. However, he could read only two: Mr. and Mrs.

These were the first abbreviations covered by our text, entirely new territory. My friend was intrigued. I wrote the four words on his tablet as he studied each.

"Well. I'll be. You meant that's all there is to them four? I never knowt why them words was written down like that. I shore seen 'em that way lottsa times, but I never knowt why they was spell'dt like that. I need'ta know this."

"That's good," I countered, "because I need to be telling you this. *This* is what I am supposed to be teaching you today. I thought you might like these four little titles, *Mr.* Caddell. Now you can go home and tell *Mrs.* Caddell what you learned in class today." He grinned as we began to tackle each. It did not take long.

Suddenly Roy's mind took another turn. I could see it in his eyes. I could *feel* it in his body posture. He had been mulling over something he wanted to say. Was he quitting? Was he mad? Had I offended him? I held my breath.

"There's one thing I don't lik'ta do," he said sternly, tapping the table.

"I don't lik'ta work on the printin' of my letters, 'cause I al-readty knowt that. I don't think I need'ta work on them anymore. Now, I knowt you think I do, Trude. . . ." He removed his glasses as he turned my way. He was ready to do battle. I never flinched.

"No, Roy. I do not. But do you know why I have repeatedly stressed this?"

"Be-cause you want me 'ta git it perfect." His was a statement of fact. The facts as he saw them.

"No. It is because I do not want you to be embarrassed any more." He looked startled. I said nothing more, nor did he. He put his glasses back on and went straight to work, satisfied. He had made his point. He had accepted mine. I let out a sigh of relief.

It was the only complaint I ever heard Roy Caddell utter.

Also today, I had brought another ten words from the list of "300 Most Frequently Used Words" from the back of my teacher workshop handbook. I had lettered each new word on familiar green cards, which Roy now reached for eagerly.

This second group included the basic words HE, WAS, FOR, ON, ARE, AS, WITH, HIS, THEY and I.

With the possible exception of AS, we had *used* these words many times in conversation. We had not written them down. Roy knew all but one by sight.

ARE was the weak link. It was one of the hardest words this man ever had to learn. Initially, he could not recognize it. He could not read it. And he stood absolutely no chance of writing it. Zero.

For two years, we fought this demon. He would have liked ARE to quietly fall off the face of the earth — or, he would have willingly pushed it, then quickly buried the evidence. Only my own tenaciousness made ARE a part of his vocabulary. This word he had to know. *This* word he had to memorize. He did so reluctantly.

Although Roy could recognize these ten words, he could not, however, spell them — either out

"EVEN IF I JIST GOT TWO 'R THREE A THEM 300 WORDTS, THAT WAS REAL IM-PORT'NT 'TA ME — I WAS BETTER OFF THAN I WAS BEFOR'. BUT IF I GOT HALF 'A THEM RIGHT, I THOUGHT I REAL-LY LEARNT SOMETHIN'. KINDA LIKE HAVIN' A LITTLE AIR IN A TIRE, 'R NO AIR: I'LL TAKE THE AIR EVER'TIME."

loud or on paper. It was still hit and miss. Correct spelling came very, very slowly. For him, it never came soon enough.

The Monday morning Hazel had spent with us, I read to them the statistic that "three hundred words make up 65 percent of all written material." They were impressed by this 65 percent figure, as was I. The fact that three hundred words could comprise so much of our English language was substantial.

But what I was slowly gleaning — each time I brought a news clipping for Roy to read, each time he wrote something down — was that three hundred words are a mere drop in the bucket.

No one writes anything of substance with a three-hundred-word vocabulary. No one reads a newspaper with a three-hundred-word vocabulary. No one reads a book of any consequence with a three-hundred-word vocabulary. No one operates well in the literate world with a three-hundred-word vocabulary.

I said nothing. Slowly, Roy was gleaning this, too. He did not need me to tell him the road was long and rocky.

As we were leaving that day, he suddenly stripped another layer from his protective shell, revealing a sharp edge to complex problems that he faced daily as he struggled to learn. This was the world from his side of the fence, none of which I would have known had he chosen not to tell me. I would not have asked. I would not have *known* to ask.

"I knowt why I wanna hurry up so, Trude," he offered as he lit his welcoming cigarette. "It's 'cause I don't wanna be asham'dt no more of what I cain't do."

He caught me off guard. It was a heart wrenching statement to which I had no immediate reply. I had not known why this man was in such a hurry. I only knew that he pushed himself hard in class. He seemed driven from within. This man wanted to learn all I could possibly teach him, as fast as he possibly could.

His sense of urgency never rudely infringed. He never said blatantly, "Why cain't we hurry up more?" His inner hopes expressed themselves as, "Let's jist keep this up." "I can come as often as ya think I need'ta." "I jist wish'dt I couldt go faster." Or, saddest of all, "If I was smarter now, you couldt teach me more. . . . If I was smarter, I couldt learnt me more." Finally, I responded to his comments.

"What if we set a goal for ourselves, Roy, to be totally finished with this first workbook in the next four or five lessons? Or certainly, if we push ourselves, by the end of the month?"

"That'd be goodt! If you think we can, I'd like that," he excitedly answered. He was tickled there was an end in sight. To him, it must have seemed like a long time coming.

We did not quite make our goal, but we did not miss it by far. We finished the first Laubach workbook on July 8.

His revealing commentary of "hurry up" was why I came three times a week for our lessons, and why I would continue to do so for as long as I possibly could. Some weeks we did better than others, for obvious reasons. Some weeks we only met once.

But, for that entire first year and most of the second, we always came back to meeting those three days weekly for two or three hours each time, because that was the way Roy Caddell liked it best. That was the time frame in which he was most comfortable. That was good enough for me.

I simply arranged my life accordingly. I know he did, too.

"I WANT'DTA MEET AS MUCH AS WE COULDT SO'S I COULDT HURRY UP 'N LEARN. THEN, IF YA QUIT 'R IF I QUIT, I'DT BE THAT MUCH AHEADT. IF THREE WEEKS A LEARNIN' WAS ALL I WAS GONNA GIT, I WANT'DT IT."

BUILDING BLOCKS

"You knowt that wordt 'bovine' you us'dt last lesson?
Well, I us'dt it on my family this weekendt 'n they
shore was surpris'dt! Now I'm learnin' them a thing 'r
two, 'n I like it!"

When Roy greeted me for our next lesson, I could see he was pleased with himself, preened like a peacock and almost strutting as he rushed up. *This* was going to be good.

"You knowt that wordt 'bovine' you us'dt last lesson?" he queried as his words spilled forth, not waiting for an answer. "Well, I us'dt it on my family this weekendt, 'n they shore was surpris'dt! Now *I'm* learnin' them a thing 'r two, 'n I like it!"

"That's great," I finally stammered. "But, Roy, *how* did you use that word?"

"Well. You toldt me it meant 'cowlike, clumsy, slow movin',' somethin' like that. So I toldt my wife 'n boy that somethin' 'roundt the place was bovine. And then I toldt 'em what it meant 'n how we'dt look'dt it up in that dic-shunary you'dt give me. They couldn't hardt-ly believe it. I shore did fool 'em. It showt'd I real-ly hadt learnt' somethin' after all. Yep, I like doin' this!" And he puffed up like a bullfrog.

This was a "Paul Harvey's Rest of the Story." We accidentally had stumbled across the word Bovine as we were flipping through his dictionary looking for another word. When I first sighted it, I distinctly recall backtracking. Bovine was a word of which Roy would have heard, one he would want to know. So, we stopped and read the few short meanings.

"Yeah. I haf heardt a this," he said taking off his glasses. "I jist never knowt it meant that." And that would have been the end of that.

Except, as we were leaving the library that same day, a rather large woman came walking towards us, in very short shorts. Neither of us commented as we passed her. After she was well out of earshot, I casually said to Roy, trying to keep a straight face at this immediate lesson parallel, "I would say that woman was rather bovine."

He nearly hit the corner of the building as he whirled around to catch a glimpse of her before she was gone.

"Why, she shore was!" he exclaimed. "Well, I'll be. So, that's howt you'd use that 'bovine' in a sentence? I like that. Now, I can go home 'n show 'em how smart I am." Which he obviously did.

He was thrilled to find so unexpectedly, a clear-cut example of a word he now knew, a word he could use. He was beginning to see tangible rewards for his efforts, rewards he could box up in his mind and carry home, to unwrap in his world.

Small incidents like this punctuated every lesson I ever had with this man. He was like a sponge, he absorbed everything. He became a catalyst. Each time we were together, I learned from him. Initially, he always felt like he was the one learning from me. This simply was not so. He was a great teacher himself, although I must admit, I had never been in a schoolyard quite like his. I liked it.

Not a day went by when I was not in absolute stitches over something he said, or the way he said it. The man was satirically funny, extraordinarily clever, and witty beyond belief. Often, the staff could hear us laughing through thick closed doors.

Roy Caddell might not have *read* with expression in his voice, but when he spoke extemporaneously, he often sounded like the home team announcer in the final game of the World Series — with both teams tied in the bottom of the ninth. Anyone would listen.

Our workbooks were now instructing us to focus on listening skills, and we did so through repetitive exercises of words beginning and ending with the

"ALOTTA THEM SOUNDTS I DON'T KNOWT, LIKE CADDELL STARTIN' W'TH A C. I WOULDN'T A KNOWT HOW'TA SPELL THAT 'XCEPT I BEEN PRACTICIN' IT F'R SIXTY-SOME YEARS. THAT C SOUND'DT LIKE A DUMB K 'TA ME. I SHORE DIN'T KNOWT THERE WAS A DIFF'RENCE IN THEM SOUNDTS. I DIN'T LEARNT NUTHIN' WHEN I WAS PRACTICIN' SAYIN' 'EM WRONG."

same sounds. I was to repeat pairs of words and Roy was to choose ones with similar patterns. These simplistic drills helped immensely with his listening skills and speech patterns, particularly word endings.

Although speech patterns were targeted now, they brought with them their own baggage. Roy Caddell was totally unaware that *every* word has a very definite pronunciation and ending sound.

Because he did not speak distinctly, he had developed the habit of slurring words and dropping endings. Slurring words was safe in the world in which he lived. Word endings simply did not exist for this man. Only seldom had he heard them growing up. He did not hear them now. They were not a part of his vocabulary.

His favorite replacement? The letter T: "learnt," "meant," "show'dt," "needt," "onc'dt," "readt," "goodt," "clos't," "knowt," "us'dt" and "wordt" — to name but a few.

Originally, I said nothing. I merely enunciated everything distinctly and mirrored his words or phrases back to him on occasion. In time he would either catch his own speech patterns or he would not. My job, stressed repeatedly in literacy training classes, was *not* to correct this man's speech. It was to teach him to read. Period.

However, countless times in reading exercises, as we were going over words — I would stop, look at Roy and laughingly say, "Excuse me, Sir. . . . What did you say? . . . What was that I heard? . . . I cannot hear you. I'm listening, and still waiting. . . ."

He caught my inference and began to enunciate his words distinctly, particularly endings. He preferred that to challenges from me, some of which were not so subtle. I would not let sloppy diction slide.

"Now listen carefully please, and tell me which of the following words *begin* alike: BIG and CUP, or COAT and CUP?"

"Ummm. COAT and CUP?"

"Yes."

"Which one of these words *begins* like NECK: NAME or KICK?"

"Ahh. NAME."

"NUT or LUNCH?"

"That first one. . . ."

"HAT or NAP?"

"Well. It ain't HAT, so it's gotta be that other one. NAP, was it?"

"Good. Now which one of these words *ends* like BOB: BIRD or JOB?" "BIB or BIRD?"

"Ahhh. JOB. Then that first one, not that bird one."

"Do BO<u>B</u> and JO<u>B</u> and BI<u>B</u> all *end* with the same sound?" I asked, carefully enunciating each ending, so he would remember them.

"Well. Yes, I'm pretty shore they do."

"What is that ending sound, Roy?"

"Ahhh . . . *buh?*"

"Perfect. Now what does that *buh* sound stand for?"

"Mmmm. That B letter, I think that's right."

"Correct. Now let me hear you pronounce that *buh* sound at the end. No glossing over here."

With each simplistic question asked, Roy's listening skills improved. He knew he needed this. He never begrudged the exercises.

"I know what you're tryin'ta do here, Trude. Them listenin' skills I needt real bad. 'Specially the soundts a them letters mixed up in them wordts, I needt'ta practice on that. It's the puttin' 'em together that's my trouble. I cain't hardt-ly get it all at onc'dt."

While these question-and-answer sessions seemed simplistic — and they were — they were helping Roy Caddell. Block by block we were building that pyramid. He stayed focused to that end. We bantered questions and answers about the beginning and ending letters of words through the balance of the first workbook and into the second, and then into the third.

The last sentence of my first teacher's manual states simply, *"It is important that no part of the lessons be omitted."* I took this literally. I omitted nothing from Laubach workbooks. I merely added . . . the world.

For Roy Caddell, another major reason he paid close attention to each question asked, was that he was slightly hard of hearing. At times I felt he was reading my lips, a good habit.

His hearing loss was minimal, or I most certainly would have insisted he be tested. But because he sat right beside me, always to my left, we never had significant problems. He simply could not hear some sounds distinctly.

Initially, I surmised that it was my own diction he had trouble catching. In reality, he had trouble catching any precise enunciation, period. Nonreaders do not enunciate words for any number of reasons: Clarity of pronunciation infers that they know a word and the letters in it. They do not. They have no earthly idea explicit sounds are attributed to *every* alphabetic letter. They might not even *know* the alphabet! Why risk exposure by trying to sound "fancy" with enuciation?

Definite speech patterns could mean someone asking them about words or meanings, or how specific words are used in sentences. Again, nonreaders could feel trapped. Concise speech could bring attention to them in public — as to correct spelling, word inflection or pronunciation, also dangerous. They will not risk it.

Multisyllable words insinuate that they have an education and, therefore, answers. Usually, they have neither. Adult nonreaders do not want their lack of knowledge exposed. Silence is better than shame.

The avoidance lists for these people are endless. For each person, there are different lists and different reasons.

Noncompetent readers do not want to stand out in a crowd. They want to blend into the masses, where their secrets will be safe. They will not brook taking chances.

Lesson Nine pointedly stressed listening skills, with relation to short vowel sounds. The workbook asked a student to identify these sounds at the beginning, middle and ends of words. My student was having trouble identifying them, period.

We concentrated on listening for these troublesome sounds in the words with which we were working. Neither of us was very good at short vowel sounds, all the more reason to practice. We did, over and over and over again for sixteen long months! Five years later, it is still about as clear as mud.

It is one thing to hear the sounds AHH, EHH, IEE, OHH, UHH. It is quite another to identify each sound with a particular letter of the alphabet. Too often, they sound exactly the same, particularly to an adult who is first learning to read.

Short vowel sounds are incredibly hard. One month into our lessons, they were inconceivably hazy. There was no clarity here, only muddy water. Years later, they are still hard for this man. Perhaps they always will be. There simply was no clear-cut line of demarcation on which Roy Caddell could hang that white hat of his.

After fighting these sounds for four years, I firmly believe long vowels should be taught first. Not just to adult nonreaders, but to every child in every school across America. Then, long vowels and short vowels become very simple: *If a sound is not long, it is very probably short.* How hard is that?

Go ahead, try it yourself. Pretend you cannot read. Then try and see if you can *guess* the correct short vowel in a given word, any word. It is a near impossibility, particularly if you happen to be a poor speller.

Those of us with education have another added benefit. We know the alphabet by rote. We think it, we live it, it is a part of our being. It is our second skin. We seldom listen to short vowel sounds.

Roy Caddell had no such luxury. He was still singing the alphabet song to insure he had all twenty-six letters in sequential order.

I elected now to address an area giving Roy Caddell great vexation: four words we used constantly in daily conversations; four words he blundered through every time we encountered them; four words every person on the face of the earth uses day in and day out — incorrectly for the most part. Roy had no idea there was a difference among them.

I knew these words would be covered in a later lesson, in another workbook, with far better instructions than perhaps I could give. But, I felt strongly that this man needed to know these words, now. So, again, I went out on a limb.

As I handed him two word cards with two words printed on each — divided and grouped according to obvious pronunciations, I said simply, "another logical progression." He nodded.

The word cards were grouped together according to sounds: KNEW and NEW; KNOW and NO.

For weeks we had been looking for words tucked inside words. It had become a familiar game. NEW was clearly contained in the word KNEW. NO was immediately visible in KNOW; so, also, was the word NOW, which Roy could easily read. We left that one alone.

Roy Caddell understood there are many concepts in the English language he did not have to like, but that he *had* to learn. These four words fell into that category. They were not among his favorites, nor would they ever be. But, he knew he needed them. So, he trudged onward, without rancor.

We began to tackle these small words, individually, collectively and, as the obvious pairs: KNEW and NEW, KNOW and NO. Roy was tentative. For him, these words spelled Trouble with a capital T. He pronounced them all *exactly* the same. In his mind, they were.

"Please read these to me," I began.

"Now, this 'un here I know," he said pointing at NEW. "'N this 'un here I know," he said pointing at NO. "But them other two?" and he shrugged his shoulders, sighing. "I ain't got no i-dear. . . ."

He never looked up. He sat there with glasses on, intently studying those two cards, looking back and forth from one to the other, and getting nowhere. He was not exasperated. He simply was not enthralled.

"Roy, there is no easy way to do this. You simply *have* to learn the difference between these groups of words. You *have* to know what each of these means and how to use them correctly in a sentence. I know our language is complex. Words like these are what make it so extremely hard for foreigners to learn English."

"Can shore under-standt that," he willingly concurred. "Now, let's see here. . . ." and we would begin again.

He could easily speak and use the four words correctly in a sentence. But, if we were talking and I stopped to ask which particular word we were then using, he would shake his head negatively. He had no answer for my question. He could not spell any of the four words, even the two he could recognize in their printed form. *How do you spell a word you do not know exists in print?* Impossible.

Thus, my friend never could have read KNEW and KNOW. It was inconceivable.

Even the pronunciation of KNEW and KNOW was initially beyond this man. Whenever he saw them in print, he simply looked at them and turned to shake his head at me. He stood no chance.

"If I cain't even say 'em, how can I write 'em? I couldn't. Not then — 'n sometimes not now. But I wanna learn 'em, ab-solutely. That's my goal. I like it when them letters soundt like they look. I don't like them invisible letters."

NEW and NO on the other hand, gave him absolutely no trouble *except* when they were coupled with KNEW and KNOW!

Then, he would very tentatively say, "NEW? Ahhh . . . NO?" when, in actuality, I was holding up the cards KNEW and KNOW for him to read back to me. He could only make a guess, *every single time.*

We practiced these words each lesson for weeks on end. First I showed him the words written in pairs. Then I showed him individual cards for each of the four. Then I asked him to tell me which word was which. At first he could not.

But slowly, gradually, hesitantly — over the course of many long weeks — Roy Caddell came to know these words. He could finally say with some confidence, "KNOW — NO" and "KNEW — NEW," whenever I held up the appropriate word cards.

The questioning tone in his voice when he read the words to me gradually dissipated. He was pleased, as was I.

However, it was not until the third week of June, when I quietly asked Roy "to please use each of these four words in a sentence," that I knew that he knew these words.

He had known this day would come. He was prepared. Without a moment's hesitation, he went straight to the task at hand. I held my breath. His four masterful sentences were. . . .

"I *knew* that."

"I'm gonna get me a *new* hat."

"I *know* I have to learn this."

"*No!*"

"YES!" I let out a whoop of joy!

"T'weren't real-ly no big deal, Trude," he said, his eyes twinkling mischievously as he reached for his hat.

The successful completion of this once disdainful task was a major milestone for Roy Caddell, and for me. His face was aglow as he broke into an incredible grin of total relief and satisfaction. He looked like he had just swallowed the canary.

It was a glorious lesson, one of my all-time favorites. It still brings a smile to my face.

TROUBLE AND EXPLANATIONS

He sharply recoiled. He so instinctively stepped
sideways from me that he literally hit the building. His
eyes registered shock and anger. I could feel his
disgust. I felt myself get clammy. He had not counted
on this. Neither had I.

June third was our one month anniversary and I looked forward to the day immensely. It was a radiant sunny morning and I felt like the whole world was rejoicing. It was to be short lived. The first question out of Roy Caddell's mouth sent me reeling.

"What does your husband do 'n what's his name?" Innocent sounding questions on the surface. Deadly underneath.

From previous conversations, I knew this man had encountered *very* unpleasant situations with lawyers and judges. The raw tone of voice in the telling of these encounters had been filled with sharp barbs, both for the men representing him and the men deciding his cases. Roy's position "on lawyerin'" was that if a man has money, he gets a good deal. No money = bad deal. He had all lawyers compartmentalized. For him, there was no middle ground. Thus, I never had told him what my husband did. He had not asked. I had not offered.

His questions today were perfectly normal ones, questions I knew would arise sooner or later. I was counting on later. I took a deep breath and kept my eyes dead ahead. *Be very careful here, Trude.*

Will Rogers, Roy was not. While he did not like many people, he disdained lawyers and judges. From his perspective, they were in a class by themselves: below the ground.

These next moments of conversation were crucial, a matter of life and death for Roy's education, for a wider window to the world. I *had* to shift his obvious negative into neutral. We had come too far and worked too hard. I did not want to lose this man now.

"Well, Mr. Caddell. . ." I began, still looking straight ahead. "My husband's name is Mike. He is a lawyer and municipal judge for the City of Muskogee, which simply means that, if someone gets a traffic ticket or has a minor violation with the law — like a citation for excessive trash on their property — they would go before my husband." I felt his movement.

He sharply recoiled. He so instinctively stepped sideways from me that he literally hit the building. His eyes registered shock and anger. I could *feel* his disgust. I felt myself get clammy. He had not counted on this. Neither had I.

"Now, Trude. I don't know 'bout them lawyers," he responded honestly. "I ain't *never* met a lawyer I like! Or a Judge! 'Cause I ain't never hadt nuthin' goodt come outta them. It's *all* been badt! It's jist that ever' now 'n again, us uned-ucat'dt people haf'ta put up w'th them.

"Now, I don't mean'ta be sayin' nuthin' badt 'bout y'ur husbandt, but I done toldt you befor' how I felt. I ain't chang'dt my mind, yet. . ." He left his sentence dangling, shaking his head with utter contempt.

"How well I understand your feelings," I laughed. "You are not alone. My husband and I have talked about this very thing many times. The group ranked number one in our country for being most disliked by the general American public are lawyers. All lawyers know this.

"The second most disliked professional group in America are doctors, which is rather sad. If a person *needs* either of these professions, they are certainly glad they know whom to call."

"You saidt that right," he countered. "If you needt one 'r the' other of them two, knowin' who 'ta call is the im-port'nt part. Now, is your husbandt a good lawyer? 'N what kinda lawyerin' does he do?" No pause for answers, he kept right on talking.

"He must be a goodt guy, 'cause you're so nice 'n he lets you come down here 'n do this f'r me." I did not laugh at his back-peddling satire.

"Roy, he does not *let* me come. I come because I want to, this is what I have chosen to do with my time. But, he is supportive of what I am doing with you and never has told me he does not want me coming to teach you. Is that what you are asking?"

He did not answer. His mind was far away in other venues, remembering omnipresent negatives he and his buddies used to spit and poke at the collective enclave of lawyers. Nothing good had been offered on a lawyer's behalf amongst the people he knew. He was not about to jump ship now.

"Trude, one thing you gotta understandt. You can*not* think one way y'ur whole life, 'n ever'body els'dt you're a-roundt think the 'xact same way — then suddenly, up 'n learnt one a them lawyers *might* be a goodt guy. You cain't do it. I ain't never heardt nuthin' but bad 'bout them two bunches, the lawyers 'n them judges. *Never!*

"Why, I don't know as I can even tell no-body now that I might know a goodt lawyer. I'd be run outta town in them feathers." I laughed heartily. He barely smiled.

"Well, Sir, if you are run out of town, I suggest you call my husband! He practices what is called General Law, which means nothing special-ized, nothing fancy. He is a good lawyer, he tries to be fair. He is also a great municipal judge. The City of Muskogee is lucky to have him.

"He is particularly good with young people. He goes to extra lengths to keep minor traffic violations off their records, so their insur-ance will not go sky high. That is, if they are willing to work off their fines, washing police cars or picking up trash, which they usually do if their parents come to court with them.

"But, the best part, for me, is that he is always willing to help *every-one* who comes before him as judge. Regardless of whom they know, or if he knows them. Regardless if they have money or not, he tries to treat them all the same. He tries to be fair, Roy. Most lawyers do. They are not, generally, bad people." What I would have given for a drink of water right then. . . .

"You shore hit the nail on the headt there! That treatin' ever'body the same. That 'n who you know is the im-port'nt-est part," he flatly stated, looking reluctantly like he might let me stay.

Fortunately, he then let the conversation lapse. *I* certainly did not pursue it! He had come for schooling, not for fighting. But oh, what I would have given to have gone home secretly with him that night, and overheard what he told his wife about class today. It would not have been about our lessons.

Ours was an interesting conversation, to say the least. All I cared was that we had averted disaster. It was a close call. Had he happened to ask his question weeks earlier, I do not know the outcome. I do not think he would have returned.

Lawyers were never mentioned again, until *he* brought up the sub-ject days later — to apologize to me. Somehow, I always shall think it was at Hazel's insistence.

"Trude. I din't mean'ta be puttin' y'ur husband in that group a lawyers the 'ther day. I'm shore there must be goodt lawyers out there somewheres. But, I ain't never met one — yet. He has'ta be the best one I *near-ly never met.*" His eyes twinkled mischievously.

Sixteen months later, when I happened to let slip that our youngest daughter was in law school, Roy sharply exclaimed, "You meant I'm gonna haf 'ta like two lawyers?" This time, we both laughed.

The man was funny. A sense of humor will carry a person a long way in life. Roy Caddell had one.

To this point in our workbook instructions, word endings meant tacking -ING onto a root word, such as JUMP and JUMPING. In addition, I had introduced -ED. JUMP and JUMPED.

"Past tense," I said. "-ED means that something happened five minutes ago, yesterday, or centuries ago. -ED means that an action took place in the past: It is not happening right now, nor is it an ongoing action." Roy understood. That -ED ending for verbs was easy for him.

Lesson Nine's focus was adding -S onto words. This one was tricky, only because my instructions never mentioned the difference between adding -S to verbs and adding -S to nouns. In point of fact, any mention of *nouns* and *verbs* had not been included in my teaching materials, to date.

Nor had the basic terminology *singular* and *plural* been referred to by name — nor *subject, predicate,* and *preposition.* Ultimately, I found the word *plural,* mentioned only once, buried toward the back of my teacher's text with no accompanying explanation. I found all such terms imperative to our studies. There was nothing wrong with Roy Caddell's brain capacity. He handled such terms beautifully. He knew he needed them.

"YOU PROV'DT YOURSELF, 'N EACH LESSON I TRUST'DT YA MORE. HOW DO YA PINPOINT WHEN YA START TRUSTIN' SOMEONE? F'R ME, IT'S A PRECAUTION THING. BEFOR' ALL THIS, I WOULDN'T HAF GIVEN YA A CHANCE, I'DA MISJUDGED YA. BUT, YA TAUGHT ME 'TA GIVE A GUY A CHANCE. THAT'S A GOODT THING IN A PERSON."

Without knowledge of these basic components of the English language, we would have been in over our heads, forever floundering. It was as though Roy should absorb -S and never question "Why?" It was as though I should be expected to teach -S and never explain the differences between verbs and nouns — singular and plural — as he wrote sentence after sentence, day after day. I opted otherwise.

"OK, Roy. When we add the letter -S to some words, that one letter makes the word *plural,* which simply means *more than one.* The root or original word here is GIRL. The plural is GIRL<u>S</u>. The root word is APPLE. The plural is APPLE<u>S</u>. BIRD — BIRD<u>S</u>." Each time I made the ending "S" sound distinctly, the thrust of our lesson. He caught it.

"That's it? Just one 'r two a them?"

"That's it. *Unless,* we are speaking of verbs. Verbs express the action in a sentence. *The girl jump<u>s</u>. The apple fall<u>s</u>. The boy run<u>s</u>. The dog yelp<u>s</u>. The man pick<u>s</u> up the bale of hay.*

"In all these cases, only one person is doing the action, so the verb requires an -S on the end. When more than one person does the action, you can pretty much leave the action word — or verb — alone.

"*Jump-jump<u>s</u>. Fall-fall<u>s</u>. Run-run<u>s</u>. Yelp-yelp<u>s</u>. Pick-pick<u>s</u>. Girl<u>s</u> jump. A girl jump<u>s</u>. Apple<u>s</u> fall. An apple fall<u>s</u>. Boy<u>s</u> run. A boy run<u>s</u>. Dog<u>s</u> yelp. A dog yelp<u>s</u>. Men pick. A man pick<u>s</u>.*

"Don't ask me *why,* Roy. It just is, and it is one of the real trouble areas of our language. It makes little sense even *after* it is explained. . . ." I waited to see his reaction. Nothing. He was, once again, "studyin'."

"Hmmm. I don't right-ly get all y'ur tellin' me, but I shore e'nuff heardt other people talk like y'ur sayin'. I just never knowt why. Now I knowt, 'n it'll come'ta me on down the road what it is y'ur tryin'ta get me 'ta learn.

"I can tell this here is real im-port'nt, Trude. It's just gonna take me some time 'ta get all this. But I can tell I shore do needt it. It'll just take me some studyin' on in my head."

Suddenly, I made a simple lesson complex. Once again, words were out of my mouth before I could catch them. This was not in our text. "But," I added instinctively, "not every word is made plural by simply adding -S. Some words, like ADDRESS, already end in the letter -S. So, we have to add an -ES to that word to make it plural. Let me borrow your legal tablet and I will show you what I mean. And exactly why."

He watched carefully as I wrote ADDRESS in the plural as both ADDRESS<u>S</u> and ADDRESS<u>ES</u>.

"The reason we add -ES," I said, pointing to the correct plural spelling, "is because the word ADDRESS already ends in the letter S. You can't just keep adding more -ssss to words like this. Where would you stop? You tell me . . . how many?"

"Yep. I can see that. This here one looks funny. Now." He aimed his pencil at ADDRESS<u>S</u>. He sat studying the words to clarify both spellings in his own mind.

"I can see that this here other one just looks, well, more better." And he turned to grin at me over his glasses. But, he had a question.

"So that -S there means more 'n one thing? More than one cow? One dog? One truck? And so does that -ES, when somethin' ends w'th it?"

"Exactly, Roy. Both -S and -ES are Endings. The plural forms of these words are written as COW<u>S</u>, DOG<u>S</u>, TRUCK<u>S</u> and ADDRESS<u>ES</u>." As I wrote each word, I repeated the plural forms while carefully enunciating their endings. -S endings were not, heretofore, in Roy's linguistics.

He repeated each word to himself, to reinforce exactly what it was he saw before him — what it was that I was trying to teach him, what he was striving to learn.

"Keep in mind here, Friend, I am not supposed to be teaching -ES endings to you now. These are not in this workbook."

"Trude. We done learnt me a bunch a things that ain't in that book there. Things I needt. I shore can understandt what it is y'ur a showin' me. But, I miss'dt it at first. It makes sense'dt now, 'n I'm real gladt you toldt me. I need'ta knowt them things. Now I just haf'ta r'member it." Which, of course, he did.

There was rarely a time after this lesson when Roy Caddell did not know that ADDRESS called for the letters -ES to be added when speaking of more than one. Nor did he forget the accompanying principle that those same two -ES letters could be added to countless nouns ending in S, O, X, Z and -CH. ADDRESS became our catalyst for four years, a vital link to what lay ahead.

Plural endings for Roy were never hard to grasp. After all, they "made't sens'dt, 'n not much a this does." The concept of -ES was simply one more rule — plus, of course, the exception to that rule — in our convoluted study of the English language.

Fortunately for both of us, this man embraced these small addendums in learning to read and write. This was why he was here. This was why he had come.

The additional "new story words" throughout the rest of our workbook included simple words that would be of tremendous help to Roy.

The words were: LIVE, LIVES, ARE, LOOKING, GIRLS, FISHING, OLIVER'S, PUP, PUP'S, PUPS, RUNS, PET, PETS, ON, STREET, GOING, BOYS, BIRDS, JUMPS, GETS, HILLS, NUMBER, NUMBERS, THEIR, TELEPHONE, NOT, TED'S, DO, HAVE, YES, MY, NO, SNAKES, VISITS, VISITING, TEN, WINGS, NEST, UNDER and NAME.

After "our" lesson on verbs and singular and plural cases, these forty words gave my friend little trouble. He tucked their respective cards away in his black satchel and patted its extra bulk proudly. In his own mind, he was making progress.

These past few lessons, we had discussed a number of words that gave my friend trouble. Two of those were BETWEEN and AMONG. We had been talking of friends as I recall. I had said you could say "BETWEEN friends" or "AMONG friends" and have two entirely different meanings, were a person using the words correctly in a sentence. He looked askance.

"It really is very simple, Roy. *BETWEEN* connotes or means two people, as in *'between* Roy and Hazel.' Two. *AMONG* means three or more, as in *'among* Roy and Hazel and Trude.' Three.

"BETWEEN-two. AMONG-three. BETWEEN-AMONG. Two or three. That's it." I looked his way in time to watch his eyebrows shoot up.

"That's all? Just two 'r three? Shore-ly I can r'member that."

"I rather thought you could," I replied grinning, "or else, I never would have brought this up. Some of this is trying to make friends with you, Sir.

"Roy, few people know the difference *between* the two words. Even fewer people can use both correctly in a sentence. But, I want *you* to know what they mean when you hear people using them, or if you see them written somewhere. This is another hallmark of education."

"I heardt 'em us'dt al-right. But, I never knowt why befor' today. I'll haf'ta start lookin' for them two words, 'cause what you say makes alotta sense'dt. Trude, *if it's at all unusual,* I need'ta experience it for myself." I obliged the man.

Any time a word or phrase, an expression or a colloquialism, came up in the natural course of conversation — if it was out of the ordinary or did not follow general rules of English — I would stop and explain it. Maybe not right then, but in the next day or two. Often Roy had heard of a chosen topic. Sometimes he had not. Regardless, he revered the discussions.

If this man could learn anything from exceptions to rules, I wanted him to have that chance. Such were tiny windows of opportunity I would not let pass us by.

Roy Caddell needed to know why things were said a certain way. He deserved to know why one way of saying something could be grammatically correct and another way, totally wrong. Exposure was what I wanted him to have. Exposure and explanations.

For too long, he had "skipp'dt over" the literate world. He had had no other choice. Now, I wanted him to see that learning to read was not an impossible dream. Hard, yes. Impossible, no.

For sixty-four long years, he had stood tottering at the edge of a harrowing precipice, knowing that one unguarded movement would send him careening into the chasm below — with no one and nothing to stop him. Sheer devastating terror.

What an unbearable burden to carry daily on stooped shoulders, for anyone of any age. A weight I could not imagine. A scarlet letter.

DAY
13

NEW ENGLAND FRIENDS

"The way I figger it, Trude, them other people know how'ta talk 'n what this is all suppos'dta soundt like. That other way a talkin' I been sayin', soundts, well, cheeper. This way soundts more high-class 'ta me."

It was hay season. From our conversations, I could tell my friend was fearful of getting his hay cut and baled, which always depended upon weather. Eastern Oklahoma had been deluged this June. Every farmer was uneasily awaiting fields to dry.

"I al-most din't come in today," he announced as soon as he was out of his truck that warm spring morning. "I start'dta call ya several times, but then I thought if I start'dt not comin' even onc't, I might get outta the habit. Now, I'm hopin' I can learn somethin'. But I al-ways do, so I don't knowt why I'd say that."

We had a full day ahead, I hoped he could concentrate.

When teachers find themselves mentally backtracking repeatedly — so as to leave nothing out, it can be very intimidating to know which area to cover first. Often we pick the first space we come to, and from there the race is on. In our case, the first squares we hit were textbook lessons. We stayed on track for weeks. But somewhere along the way, divergent subjects began vying for our attention, clamoring for recognition.

The common names of immediate family members was one such square we could not avoid.

In our last lesson, the capital letter U stood for UNCLE. Roy had problems reading the word, but eventually, he got it. The short vowel sound, U, is *very* difficult to pin-point in pronunciation, particularly for beginning readers. We were four weeks into lessons.

What I was positive Roy Caddell could not get, after watching his UNCLE struggle, was family member titles which are a distinct part of any culture. Since, initially, he could read and write somewhat, I surmised that he would know generic titles of family members. Wrong.

His approach was one size fits all. *Family* was the optimum word, and covered everyone under that umbrella. We had our work cut out for us today. These names *had* to be covered.

The words I had in mind were: MOTHER, FATHER, SISTER, BROTHER, CHILD, CHILDREN, AUNT, UNCLE, GRANDMOTHER, GRANDFATHER, GRANDPARENT, PARENT, FRIEND, FAMILY, MAN, WOMAN, BOY, GIRL, SON, DAUGHTER and the obvious plural counterparts — some easy, some hard.

With the possible exception of BOY, GIRL and now, UNCLE, Roy had no earthly idea how to recognize these words. It was not even a close vote. It was *no contest*.

My assumption was that if a student knew MAN, a student knew WOMAN. If a student knew FATHER, a student knew MOTHER. Wrong again.

Surely, I thought, everyone has an aunt or uncle tucked away somewhere, and probably a grandmother or grandfather. Yes and no. Nonreaders might have these relatives, and call them by name, but not necessarily some "fancy writin' title." I must have been living on another planet.

Our first workbook had included GIRL in Lesson 1; MAN in Lesson 2; WOMAN in 3; CHILDREN in 5; BOY in 6 and UNCLE, in Lesson 9, used as "Uncle Ted lives on York Street."

Our list of "300 Most Frequently Used Words," printed in the back of the *Tutor Workshop Handbook*, listed MAN as the first of the familial names I found. MAN ranked number 124. BOY came in at number 141; MEN, 168; MOTHER, 192; FATHER, 213; CHILDREN, 253; GIRL, 288; and FAMILY, 299.

The other family-oriented words I considered mandatory were never found listed in the study materials for the first workbook. I am not saying this was good or bad. I am only saying it did not seem best for *us* to exclude these. To me, it was another logical progression.

Initially, Roy could neither spell nor read MAN. He soon moved beyond that. WOMAN, however, stood no chance thereafter, not even with me unmistakably mouthing "WO, WO-<u>man</u>. WO<u>man</u>. Woman." Forget it. I was wasting our time.

But we could not forget these. This man had to have them — not for me, but for himself. Thus, I began hammering the words home before we made the jump into Book Two. We would not be going back to pick these up later, other than in review.

In my own mind, MOTHER and FATHER were obviously at the top of the list of necessary family vocabulary. We all have one of each, and many of us are one or the other.

We began with MOTHER. The first item covered was that the letter O in this word was a short vowel sound. "Not real friendt-ly, yet."

Next, we dealt with the digraph -TH. These two letters were at least recognizable to Roy now, no small feat. He still abhorred them.

He easily could see the tiny word HER at the end of MOTHER, and he could hear its pronunciation: mot<u>HER</u>. But the whole word together? Forget it.

The hardest part for this man was the pronunciation of the word. Twisting his mouth to form M and O at the same time was difficult. Then, toss in -TH and you have "trouble in River City."

It was not enough to me that he simply recognize this word, but that he know how to correctly pronounce it. He was capable, thus, I pushed. Twenty minutes later, he had it right.

"MO-THer."

"Again."

"Mot-her."

"Again."

"Moth-er."

"Once more, you almost have it."

"Mo-TH-her."

"What? That one threw me!"

"MoTHer."

"Yes! Again."

"MotHER. MoTHer. Mother."

Of course, Roy Caddell liked knowing this very basic word. He had a mother who was still living. Granted, she did not know yet that he was "comin'ta school 'ta learn'ta read 'n write." But, this word was important in *his* world, always my bottom line.

Repeatedly I told the man, "I do not care *how* you learn all this, only that you do. I bloody well do not care if we come in the front door or the back door of that house, as long as we get inside!" He would chuckle at my satire, but he remembered.

FATHER was not so difficult after MOTHER, but it was not a cakewalk either. The only two letters that were different were the first two, FA. Roy could not spell or recognize the word initially, but he quickly learned. With me first pointing to MOTHER, and then to FATHER and back again — repeating both the whole while — FATHER took us five minutes. The pronunciation took a little longer.

GRANDMOTHER and GRANDFATHER, I presented next. Surely they would seem easy after Father and Mother. Roy not only was a Grandfather, but he knew my marvelous ninety-six-year-old Grandfather L.R. Pilkington, who was vitally interested in Roy's progress.

GRANDMOTHER and GRANDFATHER I tackled in tandem: "You can't have one without the other." The same applied to other familial names and titles. Groups often are more readily assimilated than solos, strictly my opinion.

I just thought that GRANDMOTHER and GRANDFATHER would be easier after MOTHER and FATHER. Wrong. Roy took one look at the two words and turned to me.

"I ain't got no i-dear 'bout them two, Trude."

"Well, what if we break the double word GRANDMOTHER apart, and see what we have." I underlined both GRAND and MOTHER, and then wrote both separately on another line of his yellow legal tablet. Still, he was absolutely bumfuzzled. I was surprised.

"Trude, I knowt what y'ur tryin'ta do here. It jist ain't takin' yet. I needt some help." He continued to glance from one to the other, and back again.

"Roy, what if we take GR from this first word GRAND. What word would we have?" I covered the first two letters with my fingers.

"And?" he soberly asked, none-too-sure of his answer.

"Yes. AND. Now, what sounds do the two letters GR make? GR is a consonant blend that works together. What would you have?"

"Grrr?"

"Yes. Grrr. Now, put the two together and what do you have?"

"Grrr-and?"

"Yes. Say it faster, as one word."

Slowly he got it, but it was not easy. None of this was. When we then rebuilt the word GRANDMOTHER from GRAND and MOTHER, it finally hit him. He was genuinely surprised, yet disappointed with himself. "A cours't. I shouldta knowt that."

Which was absolutely untrue. *There was nothing about any of this that he* "shouldta knowt!"

Few nonreaders try to dissect words by themselves — the frustration level is too great. To them, many words are beyond their abilities. Even simple words are complex. Thus, there is safety in avoidance.

For my friend, such a solo undertaking of reading and/or spelling these words was out of the question. It would have been too degrading, which was why we tackled them together. More failure he did not need.

"I done tri'dt this myself, Trude. Lots a times ov'r the years. I couldt *not* get it a-lone. I had'ta haf me some help w'th them things, 'cause I give up long ago on ever gettin' it myself."

Needless to say, after spelling GRANDMOTHER, GRANDFATHER was a cakewalk. Here though, I was too good to Roy — I did not ask him to spell PILKINGTON!

We trudged on through the other familial words slowly: SISTER, BROTHER, CHILD, CHILDREN, PARENT, GRANDPARENT, AUNT, UNCLE, MAN, WOMAN and FAMILY.

With each word conquered, his grin widened. He knew what these commonplace words would mean to him. His world was widening, and he loved it. He needed it. Today, whenever Roy Caddell hears people talking about their family members and relatives, he feels free to join the conversation, if he so chooses.

"In my past life, there woulda been *no ways!*"

Gradually, over the course of many weeks, I had noticed that Roy Caddell was speaking better grammatically. I could hear subtle, definite changes in his diction, in how he expressed himself, how he put words together, his sentence structure. Syntax.

Granted, if he were agitated, he quickly reverted to old, familiar patterns. But when he was relaxed, I could easily perceive changes. Some were more pronounced than others, but all were obvious.

For one, he had begun to correct himself, which amazed me. For another, his speech was becoming more distinct and grammatically correct. There was not so much slang. I do not think Roy was aware of this initially, so I said nothing for the longest time. When I finally did, his response was simplistic.

"The way I figger it, Trude, them other people know how'ta talk 'n what this is all suppos'dta soundt like. That other way a talkin' I been sayin', soundts, well, cheaper. This way soundts *more high-class 'ta me.*" I nearly fell out of my chair!

This change in Roy's diction, I had not expected. Probably because I had never tutored before. But for a man to change speech habits at the age of sixty-four, was significantly impressive to me.

From his perspective, all he had ascertained of his diction was that he "soundt'd hillbilly." I explained that he did not sound so to me. I thought he sounded more "country." In every area of our nation, people speak with different dialects that are unique to the geographic region in which they live, or were raised.

"It is called colloquialism, Roy. If you think you sound funny, you should hear the people in New England talk. They speak through their noses, and we in the south can barely understand them . . . nor they, us. PAAArk y'ur CAAAh," I slowly said, as I held the bridge of my nose. He got my meaning and grinned.

I cannot recall a single time when I corrected this man's diction, per se, unless he specifically asked me how something was said. My job was to teach the man to read, period. Whatever else ensued would be strictly an added bonus.

Three years later, when Roy and I were speaking about his limited language idioms — the words and phrases he reiterated in those early weeks and months of schooling — he freely admitted that "my vo-cab-ulary was narrow back then, Trude. I only knew how'ta say the same words ov'r and ov'r. That was all I knew.

"I'm standin' here now lookin' at me in my mind's eye back then. . . I musta really been somethin'."

That you were, Mr. Caddell. You were my high-class friend who could never be from New England.

THE WALLS OF JERICHO

*"You know, mosta the time I feel haf-badt when I gets
here. I'm haf-scair'dt I'm not gonna learn anythin', 'n
haf-scair'dt we're not goin' fast e'nuff. I'm al-ways
scair'dt I'll miss somethin' I real-ly need'ta learn, only
I won't know 'bout it 'til it's too late. But, no matter
how bad I feel when I gets here, I al-ways feel great
when I leave."*

It looked like *Henny Penny* outside: The sky was ready to open wide at
any moment to dump its load. As soon as I was out of my car, Roy asked
flatly, "Is it al-right if we don't stay too long today? My son ask'dt me 'ta
help him cut sum'a his hay, and I hate'ta turn him down. I start'dta call
'n ask if we couldt just not meet today, but I don't like not to come. I *need*
this. I don't wanna get outta the habit." Roy Caddell looked worried
and weary. Both concerned me.

"What say we don't meet next time, or any day you need. You con-
centrate on getting that hay cut, and I will wait until I hear from you to
start again." He smiled his thanks, nodding.

By now, we were ensconced in our familiar seats upstairs, though we
would stay but a minute. My friend's odds for cutting hay did not look
good. He was clearly pressed for time.

From conversations, I had gleaned that "haying" is no simple
process. It is complicated business, with tractors breaking down and
parts not readily accessible. It is trips into town when you do not have
the time. It is a convoluted exercise that too often is futile.

It did not matter to me if we did not meet for these next days, or
weeks. It obviously did to him.

"Trude. I'm al-ways afear'dt I'm gonna forget ever'thing we've
learnt here when we don't meet like we're suppos'dta. I cain't afford

that. I *needt* ever' little thing you tell me. Fact is, I need'dt it yesterday, but I'm havin'ta settle on today."

So that was why. This man had no idea how smart he was. He forgot nothing. His comprehension skills were incredible, as was his retention.

"Now," he impishly grinned as he fished inside his satchel, "my wife said'ta give you this."

This was a list of the capital letters of the alphabet, written legibly down the left-hand side of a sheet of legal paper, in Hazel's handwriting. *For me!* My mouth flew open.

"She weren't too sure 'bout sendin' this, but I ask'dt her to write down all a them letters f'r you. I toldt her you'dt be real glad'ta have 'em. You needt this now, Trude. Hazel writes goodt 'n can help you w'th your writin', anytime." He loved playing teacher.

"Now," he said grinning, "*your* homework is'ta go home 'n practice writin' like this sheet. Ya been wantin' some letters to copy, now you got 'em. Next time *I'll* check homework, 'n then take it home for Hazel to grade't."

Was this the real reason he had driven into town today? I only could wonder, and feel awful if it were.

Quickly, I pulled out more cards of Roy's Words: MANURE, FEED LOT, CHICKENS and VETERINARIAN.

MANURE was the only word he could not read, which rather surprised me. Although we had not covered the -URE ending, I had not expected trouble. Those three letters threw him. The MAN part, he easily recognized. Once we broke the word apart into syllables, and put the components together again, he had it.

Even though VETERINARIANS are a vital part of Roy Caddell's world, I had not thought he would recognize that word. Foolish me.

"But," he freely admitted, almost reading my mind, "I couldt not come close'ta spellin' that wordt befor' today. It shore e'nuff soundts like it looks. It even looks like it soundts. Hmmm. . . ."

"I looked it up myself this morning to be sure I had spelled it right. This word, Roy, spells *exactly* like it sounds when we break it down into syllables. Syllables are the key. *Vet-er-i-nar-i-an*. Vet-er-i-nar-i-an," I repeated.

"But . . . to be positive, let's look it up in *your* dictionary." He reached reluctantly into his zipped compartment to pull the book out, to begin looking painstakingly for the Vs. It took some time to find them.

Only months later did I learn that those first few weeks Roy repeatedly told his wife, "You don't *never* say a wordt 'round Trude you don't know, 'r you're gonna haf'ta get out that dic-shunary. 'N you better not say a wordt unless you can spell it! She'll haf you lookin' it up in that thing, ever' time." I loved his satire, especially since I knew he merely tolerated my admiration "f'r that there book."

Spelling was becoming crucial to this man. Roy felt spelling was the magic key to obtaining all he lacked. He was utterly convinced he needed to know *exactly* how to spell every single word we came to as we traveled through our workbooks. My theory was ultimately, yes; now, no.

At this point, I felt strongly that Roy Caddell had more than enough, not only in class, but in responsibilities outside. I did not want him overloaded. But, since the "spellin' of all them wordts" was important to him, it was important to me. I took our familiar Back Door Approach.

"Let's look at this another way," I offered as a compromise. "The more you see these words, the more you will come to recognize if they are *not* spelled correctly. That helps me. Often, I cannot tell *how* to correctly spell a word, even when I repeatedly sound it out. But, I can usually tell when it is *not* spelled correctly. That is when I have to reach, again, for my dictionary.

"No one knows it all, Sir. That is why we constantly see people inside this library. They need help. You, Mr. Caddell," I said, "happen to have your own private tutor for finding answers!"

"Yeah. Maybe so. I am gettin' now so's I can sorta tell by lookin' at sum'a them words if they aren't spell'dt right. But I still got me a long ways to go."

"Don't we all, Roy. Don't we all. . . ." We went back to work.

From out of nowhere, Roy brought up a topic that really was none of my concern. His admission startled me.

"I got after my boy the other day. He took down a phone message real sloppy-like. I toldt him it don't take no more time to do it right. I surpris'dt him, but I meant it." He let the topic lapse as I sat silently.

Suddenly it hit. *Control!* Roy Caddell was afraid of losing control in his world, which was rapidly shifting around him without permission. *He* was changing, which meant everything in his household was changing. It was surely a frightening prospect for each member of the family.

"Control" had been spoken of in literacy training classes, but I had not given the matter much thought. Once again, hearing words and seeing feelings are two vastly different creatures.

Humans, like animals, often strike out in fear if their territory is being invaded. My friend was fearful. He simply did not know how to tell me other than as he did. Some change he could stand, as long as *he* held the reins.

I took a deep breath and held my tongue. This was neither the time nor the place to respond to potentially dangerous thinking. He would either see the folly of his attitudes, or he would not. I was not his guardian. I was his friend. Therefore, I listened.

He paused before he went on, initially speaking more to himself than to me. He was about to open another Pandora's Box.

"You know, there's one thing I don't understandt," he said softly, "why ever'one who cain't readt don't come 'n ask f'r help, to learn all this. To me, it's been a goodt thing. I like comin' here. But I'd shore think ever'one couldt do this *if they just want'dt to.*"

He was very definite on this opinion. He had given the matter its due consideration, from his vantage point.

"MY SON HADT HIM AN ED-UCASHUN, 'N I WANT'DT HIM 'TA USE IT, 'CAUSE I WAS FEELIN' BADT THAT I COULDN'T WRITE DOWN A MESSAGE. BACK IN THEM OLDEN DAYS, I CAN R'MEMBER I WAS THE LAW. I MEANT IT GOODT, BUT I SEE NOW ALOTTA IT CAME OUT BADT."

There was a mindset in Roy Caddell that scared me, for him. He had a narrowness to his thinking that he spoke of openly and often: "I done toldt Hazel I ain'ta gonna change. I ain't changin' 'n that's that!" Or, "I like the way I am. I done pret-ty goodt by it so fars. I'm stickin' w'th it."

He had done well, unbelievably so. But, such thinking is defensive. It can back a person right into a corner they will fight to the death to defend, without once considering that they might be wrong.

His last comment, on why nonreaders such as himself, were not flocking to public libraries in droves to learn how to read, I could not let slide. I took a very deep breath.

"Well, Roy, I cannot agree with your statement and I will tell you why." He whirled around to face me. *This* he had to hear.

"So many many people do want to learn to read. They do not want to remain illiterate all their lives. You did not. They do not.

"But, what if they are married to people who also cannot read and write? What if their spouse does not *want* them to come and learn this? Who, then, is going to encourage them to learn to read and write? Who is going to care? Rather than meeting with constant positives, they would meet with bitter negatives, and maybe even real unkindness.

"Or, what if they do choose to come to learn, but they do not have regular transportation like you do? They always would have to be asking and depending on others to get them to class, and on time. Most people would soon become very uncomfortable with that. I know I would.

"Or, what if they have small children at home? Who would take care of those little ones on class days? What if those children suddenly became sick on class days, who would care for them?

"Or, what if these people had no telephone, and had to walk blocks or miles to call and cancel their class session for that day. Would they simply not show up, and leave their instructor hanging?

"Or, what if they do have a car, but it won't start? Or, let's compound that — what if they also have no telephone they can use to call their teacher? What then?

"Roy, we have been told that if a student does not call to cancel a lesson, or simply does not show up three times in a row, we no longer have an obligation and responsibility to try and teach that student. We can end the lessons right there and then. . . . We can be the ones not to show up the next time." I paused to let this sink in. His eyes registered shock.

Never once had he entertained the notion that I could end our lessons. Why should he? This did not apply to us, thus I never had mentioned it. Since he was speechless, I continued.

"Or, what if someone wants to learn to read, like you do. But, what if there is no money available to do this, not one extra red cent. Not gas money. Not money to buy workbooks. Not money for babysitters. Not money for *anything*. What would you suggest they do then, Mr. Caddell?

"Or," I added for closure, "What if no one else in a family ever helps these people? You have Hazel and your entire family behind you, or at least the ones you have chosen to tell. Hazel is *always* asking how she can help. You are supported one thousand percent.

"But, can you fathom how you would *feel* if no one truly cared if you learned to read or not? If they only gave lip service to your wishes and, in fact, undermined you at every turn?

"How long do you think you would keep this up if you had very many of these obstacles to contend with, Sir?"

You could have heard a pin drop. The man was immobile. For a long time, he sat looking at the table and shaking his head. The realization of his situation hit home, like a thunderbolt. It was as if he had been hit in the head with a baseball bat.

Seldom are things totally black or white, or as they appear. Here were irrefutable facts with which he could identify, and which he could not ignore. Here was his world, outlined in brilliant color and in 3-D. Finally, he slowly spoke, his voice not above a whisper, his eyes still down.

"I see what you mean. Ever'thing you say makes perfect sense't. I just never hadt look'dt at it that way befor'.

"First off. You haf'ta wanna do this. And I do. Next off. Someone has'ta encourage you, 'n I've got that in my wife 'n my boy. And you. Third off, you gotta haf a good teacher. I've got that, too. I *am* one of the lucky ones, I am."

Certainly, I had not meant to get into this today. He did not have the time — his hay was waiting. But, I had learned that when Roy Caddell brought up a topic he wanted to talk about, we talked. Then. He revered stimulating discussions. He certainly had not been disappointed today!

It was a powerful lesson. We never opened a book. We stayed just under fifty minutes. The rest of my planned lesson would have to wait. We were gathering our things to leave when he very pensively revealed, "You know, mosta the time I feel haf-badt when I gets here. I'm haf-scair'dt I'm not gonna learn anythin', 'n haf-scair'dt we're not goin' fast e-nuff. I'm al-ways scair'dt I'll miss somethin' I really need'ta learn, only I won't knowt 'bout it 'til it's too late.

"But no matter how bad I feel when I gets here, I al-ways feel great when I leave. It's been a goodt day. I'm real gladt I came, Trude. Thank you." And he tipped his white hat my direction.

As I looked back on this particular panorama in the months and years that followed, I always believed that this was the moment when the outer parameters of Roy Caddell's mindset began to crumble.

And, "The Walls Came a Tumblin' Down."

THE
"FLUTTERIN' TRUCK"

*"What I real-ly wanna do, is 'ta
getta the place'dt where, when
som'body asks me what I do, I
can tell 'em I'm comin' down
here three days a week 'n workin'
on my ed-ucashun. I wanna get
so's I'm not em-barrass'd'ta tell
people I'm comin' here 'cause I
cain't read 'n write so goodt."*

Roy cancelled two lessons in early June because of his hay. He was under tremendous strain. Then I received a message that sounded like ten tons had been lifted from him. Once again, I heard a lilt in his voice. "Trude. This is Roy. I'm plannin'ta be there tomorrow, I gotta check y'ur homework." Yow!

I had to get behind the proverbial eight ball, and fast. I had not attempted to emulate Hazel's beautiful printed alphabet. I was up at six-thirty the next morning to finish both those and my lesson.

It took me thirty minutes alone to fill one page in a yellow legal tablet as I laboriously copied the twenty-six letters she had kindly written out. I had not done this in years and, quite frankly, I needed the practice. I did get better as I wrote each repeatedly. Perhaps I would get a passing grade. Only time would tell.

"WHEN I COULDT BE HELPIN' YOU W'TH Y'UR WRITIN', THAT LET ME KNOWT THAT OTHER FOLKS WEREN'T PERFECT NE'THER. IT ALSO SHOW'DT ME THAT YOU WOULDN'T LET NUTHIN' GET BY."

Then I set to work on a task that was to require a huge block of time. I am very slow and methodical about many things, this was one. I had told Roy at our last lesson that the "next time we meet, we are going to make sentences out of all those word cards I've made for you." He had raised his eyebrows and grinned.

"Now *that* soundts in-terestin'. I'd like that." Of course, he would remember.

Subsequently, I had a *massive workload* to trudge through before our nine o'clock lesson. For me to be totally prepared today, I had to go back through previous lessons to check for story words I had missed. There were a number, and I made cards for each. I made cards for the third group of ten from the "300 Most Frequently Used Words" from which we had been working. The list included: WORDS, BUT, NOT, WHAT, ALL, WERE, WE, WHEN, YOUR and CAN.

However, the hardest part of preparing for the day was that I needed to correctly date the word cards I had made over the past six weeks. This would be the last time I would have possession of them. Sadly, I had not dated the earliest ones. Was I ever sorry, a thousand times over! It took me almost two hours to backtrack on these alone.

The lesson I had planned for this June fifteenth was to be a monumental one for us. I *had* to be ready. I barely made it.

Roy was waiting for me as I pulled up, grinning from ear to ear as he pushed that white hat back from his head. "Boy howdy now, I shore am glad'ta be back, I've miss'dt this."

"So have I, Mr. Caddell," I said giving him a hug. "Have I got something to show you! What did you say on my recorder?"

"You meant 'bout today? Your homework! You brought them letters back! Hazel will be real gladt 'cause she ask'dt about 'em. She toldt me to be nice to you 'n help you w'th 'em all I couldt." He smiled mischievously.

He was anxious to get upstairs to see my elemental attempts at decent penmanship. This would be a real role reversal for us. But, homework is homework — his, or mine.

Gingerly, I handed him my offering. He sat there for several minutes, intensely studying what I had written. Finally, he smiled.

"You done goodt here, Trude. These are a whole lot better than what ya been makin'. Ya got mosta them letters wrote so's I can tell what they are. But I cain't hardt-ly believe *my teacher is a studyin'*. I real-ly gots me somethin' 'ta tell someday." *Me, too, Mr. Caddell. Me, too. . . .*

"Ya knowt," he continued in all earnestness, "it's hard'ta change a habit like you're doin' here. And I knowt you're tryin' 'cause I can see where you got better as you went along down the line.

"Onc'dt we're thru learnin' you this, Trude, you're gonna be able to write both fast and neat. You'll do good if you keep this up. It's shore better than what you been doin'."

Before we began our sentence building project, I wanted to unload the eight or ten sacks of word cards I had brought back to him.

"Fortunately for me — not you, Mr. Caddell, I *finally* have dated these. I do not need them back. In fact, I do not ever *want* them back. Perish the thought! For your future reference, though, they are all grouped as we have studied them, lesson by lesson."

"Do I need'ta leave 'em in any set order, from here on?"

"No. They are yours to do with as you wish, but I do not suggest throwing them out. We are going to be surprised at how many there actually are here. If you will please spread these out over the table, we will see what we have. The one thing I want you to keep in mind here is exactly how many words you actually *know*. It's staggering!"

"I'll tell you what now, Trude. We got an awful lotta words here. . . ." His eyes were as big as saucers as he opened each bulging sack carefully.

It took us fifteen minutes to scatter the cards across the table, then count them. Roy was stupefied. He kept putting cards out — and putting cards out. I, too, was amazed at what was unfolding, and I had known what was coming.

"Why don't you let me finish with these, while you begin counting. . . ." Bad mistake. He started and quickly lost track. I did not want my friend becoming frustrated as we were about to get this gala under way. I had him count them in groups of twenty.

"If you will turn over every twentieth card you come to, we will be able to realize what we have before us. I never dreamed we had this many, Roy. . . ." He started again, and easily got through.

"One, two . . . twenty. One, two . . . forty. There's a hundred. Twenty . . . forty . . . sixty. . . . There's two hundred. Twenty, twenty-one, twenty-two, twenty-three. I count two hundred 'n twenty-three. Boy."

Neither of us had ever once considered the number of words we were learning week by week. But, two hundred and twenty-three? *That* took my breath!

Here we stood, two ordinary people, beside a table which now totally was covered with little green cards. It was a gorgeous sight! I was sick I had not thought to bring my camera today, what a picture we would have had. We must have looked like two kids playing school . . . . We were.

"Well, Friend, are you ready to make some sentences?" His face lit up immediately. He was more than ready for this day which, in actuality, would be the first time he would attempt sentences on his own, without dictation from me. He was fairly confident he could do this. I was *very* confident he could.

"I think I am. I toldt Hazel this mornin' we was gonna do this today. So we spreadt all them little cards out you give me, 'n I made't up some sentences. Mine had the woman yellin' at some snake." Glad to know he had used his favorite word.

Randomly, I picked out cards to make the first sentence: A RIVER IS IN THE VALLEY. Roy did the honors next: THE MAN LOOKS AT THE SNAKE. HE YELLS.

"Great. You made two sentences, I made one," I said as I looked at his beaming face.

My second sentence was: IT IS A MAN. Roy's was: HE "GET" THE BOY'S APPLE. We did not have cards for the words GOT or GETS, or even the letter -S. My mistake.

"What," I offered, searching the table and reaching for a card, "if we use this word SELLS in place of the word GET here, Roy." He knew why immediately.

"'Cause GET ain't right, is it? It should have an -S on it, should'nt it?" He knew that GET did not *sound right* in this sentence.

"Correct. Remember what I've told you about subjects and verbs? That a singular subject always must have a singular verb, and a plural subject requires a plural verb. Your sentence is a perfect example of that very definite rule." He shook his head in understanding.

We had discussed this weeks before, though only casually. Roy remembered the terms and understood the concept well enough to know his sentence was not grammatically correct. I would take it any way he learned it.

"Your sentence, to be grammatically correct, should read: HE SELL<u>S</u> THE BOY'S APPLE. Or, HE GET<u>S</u> THE BOY'S APPLE, if only I had made an -S for us."

"I see. I know what you're sayin'. I can *hear* the difference when I listen 'n you show me all this. Now I see why you been tellin' me them things. It makes a difference, it shore do."

"Trude. That sentence I used earlier, it shouldt have been DOESN'T, shouldt'nt it?" He raised his eyes to mine to see if I was following his train of thought. I stood there pensively, trying to recall exactly to what it was he was referring. Then it clicked. Moments earlier he had said, "It just *don't* soundt right."

"Yes, Roy. You are exactly right, but how in the devil did you figure that out? The correct way, using proper grammar, is to say 'It *doesn't* sound right.'" This pointed grammatical subject never had come up in our conversations, and I am not sure I had thought it ever would, certainly not in this first workbook.

"Well, I guess I'm gettin' pretty smart. I been listenin' to how people talk. And I'm beginnin' to pick up on the difference. Only problem is, I'm not aroundt all that many people that talk that way."

"The ones that do," and he paused making a face as if he did not quite know how to say this without offense, "they soundt, well, al-most funny. I don't know as I couldt use that word aroundt country folk. I don't think I couldt go to town 'n talk fancy like that. They'd think I'd gone plum loco." He smiled wistfully.

All this in the middle of sentence building, over the word DOESN'T. Oh, my. . . . Roy saw my perplexity.

"Trude, I went all my life tryin'ta pick up on them fancy words other people use. I needt this. I'd just as soon talk the way I'm suppos'dt to, what soundts right. Where before. . . ." His voice trailed off as he silently shrugged his shoulders.

Here I stood, listening to an account of a surreal world, trying to steady myself. Finally, I found my voice.

"Oh, Roy. I hope I am helping you in your world. I know so many of these words, like FLUTTERED, you will probably never use. But an awfully lot of them, you will use all the rest of your life." I did not know what else to say.

"Well now," he said grinning broadly, "I don't know 'bout that. Why, just the other day my truck was a flutterin'. I thought of that word FLUTTERED we readt in that story 'bout the little fox. That's what my truck soundt'd like, a bird flutterin'. So you see, Trude, all this *is* a helpin' me, 'n I'm real gladt I'm doin' it."

Yes! I felt my heart soar. At that moment, Rachmaninoff could not have moved me more. The man was eloquent. His syntax was lyrical, almost magical. He had a gift and I knew it, from Day One. He did not.

We continued with our task at hand: Sentence construction. Roy made one I especially remember: IT IS <u>AN</u> EGG. From myriad conversations, he distinctly remembered to use the word AN before words beginning with a vowel. This, too, was huge progress. Then I threw in another clinker.

"Roy. We talked of verbs a moment ago. The word IS that you used in your last sentence IT IS AN EGG, is called a *linking verb*. It connects or links the two parts of a sentence together, like a bridge. And it does it *every single time*. The word IS links your subject with what follows. Your sentence is a perfect example of a linking verb and its usage." He was listening intently.

"Both IT and EGG, or APPLE or ORANGE, or whatever the heck you want to use, can be interchanged. Your sentence could also read: THE EGG IS IT; THE APPLE IS IT; THE ORANGE IS IT. Or, conversely: IT IS AN EGG; IT IS AN APPLE; IT IS AN ORANGE. Take your pick of how you say it, either way is correct.

"Other linking verbs are AM, IS, ARE, WAS, WERE, BE, BEING and BEEN. I still remember memorizing these years ago in school. Every child learns linking verbs in schoolhouses across America, year in and year out. We cannot operate without these tiny verbs."

"You mean, w'th sum'a them verb things there, I can switch things aroundt? Trade 'em, one f'r the other?"

"That is exactly what I mean. I know I am not supposed to be telling you this now. I do not mean to confuse you. I am honestly trying to help, Roy, so when these come up in another workbook, you at least will have heard of them." Standing there, he kept "studyin'" the table. I waited. Finally, he turned.

"Makes sense't, what you're tellin' me. But I'da skipp'dt over them words I din't know w'thout my doin' this here. Then I'da gotten mad. I done that a bunch over the years. I still do at times. But, I'm gettin' better 'bout that, too. Now, I'm at least tryin'ta figure out summa this f'r myself. It's all a helpin'." We turned our attentions back to our lesson.

From our ocean of words, I made dozens of sentences in staccato order, reaching across the table for words I needed. I borrowed some words from sentences we already had made.

The last sentence I remember making was THE HAY BALER IS IN THE BARN. I distinctly recall this one because, immediately, we started substituting words for HAY BALER. Roy caught on quickly.

First, we substituted MOWER. Next, POST HOLE DIGGER. Then, TRACTOR. Suddenly he said, "I guess't we could say THE LADY IS IN THE BARN. THE BABY IS IN THE BARN. THE CATTLE IS IN THE BARN."

"Close . . . but, not quite. Let's repeat that last one again, and then you tell me how it should read."

"Ummm, oh, yeah. It shouldt say THE CATTLE ARE IN THE BARN. 'Cause CATTLE is more than one cow, it takes one a them other verbs.

"I guess, Trude, you couldt put anythin' you want'dt to IN THE BARN, *if you hadt the right words.*" I was, once again, astounded.

Not Roy. He was grinning from ear to ear. By his bright expression, I could see he had just zeroed in on key elements within our language. Because he listened in minute detail, sentences suddenly had become FACT to Roy Caddell. No longer were they an enigma in thin air, always beyond his grasp. Already today, our time had been well spent.

We attacked the disaster area again, we were not finished. We had been at this over two hours now, but we still had "miles to go."

"These last sentences you made are clear examples of linking verbs: THE COW IS IN THE BARN; THE CATTLE ARE IN THE BARN. Both IS and ARE are. . ."

". . . them linkin' verbs," Roy chimed in.

"You got it. The parts of your sentence need one another, Roy, like words and people do. We are right back to Square One: None of this is any good without the other."

"Yeah. I r'member you tellin' me that. It made sense't then. It shore makes sense't after this. I think I'm comin' to the point where I'll be r'memberin' more 'n more of what it is you're a tellin' me. But, I ain't there yet.

"What I really wanna do, is'ta getta the place'dt where, when som'body asks me what I do, I can tell 'em I'm comin' down here three days a week 'n workin' on my ed-ucashun. They think I'm a bum now 'cause I don't work no regular job. But I don't care 'bout that so much 'cause I know it ain't so.

"But this here," he said, definitively thumping the table, "I care about. I wanna get so's I'm not em-barrass'd'ta tell people I'm comin' here 'cause I cain't read 'n write so goodt. . ." His voice trailed off along with his thoughts.

I did not know who *they* were. I did not ask, as it did not matter to me. Thankfully, it sounded like it did not matter to him. However, it would be another four years before this man could publicly acknowledge his reading deficit.

It was through Roy Caddell that I became acutely aware of the arch nemesis that shadows every nonreader: Shame. Not one person who cannot read does not live without the constant and dreaded fear of exposure. That relentless and unwanted companion continually leaves stomachs and lives in knots, all the while quietly whispering:

Never let down your guard. Always look over your shoulder. Laughter and ridicule lie just ahead. Forget Feelings. There is only Anger, Disappointment, Exclusion, Sorrow and Embarrassment. I told you so. . . . I warned you. . . . Na-na-na-na-na-na.

No wonder people walk around with sad faces. We see them every day, you and I. Faces mirror lives, and pain. How selfish of me not to have recognized that this also could be attributed to someone who cannot read. How grateful I was to my friend for awakening me to cold hard facts from a world I never would have known. Always I will say, of the two of us, this man is the better teacher.

As we collected our cards to leave that day, I looked over at Roy from across the table and said, with a twinkle in my eye, "OK, Friend. I want to hear you pronounce our favorite word."

He hesitated but a split second, his own eyes twinkling in return. His white hat stayed suspended in mid-air while he completed the honors. "ROOO-MP."

"Yippee!" I yelled. "You got it! Hooray! Hooray!"

"Yeah. I think I fi-nally got that one down right. 'Bout time, too — I been practicin'. I *knew* you was gonna ask me that today. This here's been a really goodt lesson, Trude. Thank you."

My pleasure, Sir. It had indeed been a good day, one that would live in our memories. It was a day when Roy Caddell's infamy was chiseled away. Stone by stone.

He put on his hat and we walked out the door.

To, Too and Two

Slowly but surely, he began to feel better about himself,
to walk taller, to nod that white hat of his toward
others, even to smile on occasion. Simply because he
could read! Maybe not everything, but something!
And for someone like Roy, something can be
everything, and is most definitely better than nothing.

Structure fascinates me, whether in buildings or sentences. Perhaps I am a latent architect of both. Word composition and construction are passions. They became building blocks for a lifetime for Roy Caddell.

One of the things I had repeatedly observed was, that while he could read some things, he could write little other than simple words and phrases — and not always those.

When we first began our lessons, he had no idea sentences begin with capital letters and end with punctuation, the most basic of tenets. Slowly, I came to comprehend why reading and writing are taught as one unit. A student cannot read if they cannot write. Roy could not. All teachers know this. Originally, I did not.

My first inkling of a writing deficit was that Roy did not write lists for running errands. Hazel did. He did not write checks. Hazel did. He did not write birthday cards. Hazel did. He did not write his commentary on "How Learning to Read Has Opened My World." Hazel did.

But he drew pictures that only he could decipher. They were raw and they were primitive, but stick figure drawings worked for him. He had devised a simplistic sign language all his own. Up to this point, that was all that mattered in his world.

At this particular lesson in mid-June, I decided that we had danced around this issue long enough. We would address this deficiency Roy Caddell felt within himself. There is nothing so impressionable as actually *doing* something for ourselves, that forever after leaves its indelible imprint stamped upon our memories. I wanted my friend to have such a memory, now.

"Roy, I want you to write me a letter please." He whirled around to face me, nearly dropping his glasses.

"Me?" he exclaimed.

"Yes. You." I calmly stated and smiled, looking around the room to see if there were another warm body for this project. There was not. He did not smile back.

"But, Trude. You know I ain't never wrote no letter befor'."

"No. But at one time, you also had never read a story. You did great with that. You will do great with this, too." I looked him dead in the eye. He knew there was no way out.

"If you say so." Reluctantly, he pulled his tablet out, turning until he found a semi-blank page. He sounded none-too-happy with this sudden writing prospect. Hrmph.

"This, please, is what I want you to write."

"Dear Trude, Thank you for teaching me to do this. I like coming down here. I have learned a lot. I am getting smarter. I think, or so you tell me, that I know more than I'm giving myself credit for. I'm going to start believing this, too. Love, Roy" He waited, pen poised.

"Now," I said. "You start writing here," and I pointed to the red left-hand margin line running the length of the page.

"DEAR goes right here."

"Here?"

I nodded. He wrote and looked up. I spelled TRUDE out for him — the spelling is tricky, he had written it only one other time.

"Now, because you are addressing someone by name, you must put a comma right after TRUDE. That is grammatically correct in letter writing." He wrote both in the right place and looked up again for further instructions.

Before he wrote the first word of the message, I told him, "Drop down to the next line and indent, or come over like you do when you start a new paragraph"

"You mean over here?" he asked incredulously.

"Yes, there. This is what we have seen in workbook stories. Only in those, they skip a line between paragraphs. In letter writing and in books, they usually indent before they start writing. It is an important use of white space that makes reading easier for the reader or the recipient of a letter."

This was news to him. He began the first sentence as I slowly repeated it. He got as far as TEACHING before he looked up for help.

"T-E-C-H?" he pensively asked.

"Close. But, not quite. There's a middle letter in there that you do not hear. It is silent. Watch my mouth and listen very carefully: TeAching. Teach-ing. Teaching."

"A?" he correctly guessed the first time.

"Yes. A silent *A*."

"T-E-*A*-C-H-ing?" he rather assuredly asked. I nodded. He went on to write the word methodically. He continued as I slowly dictated sentences. When he got to the word COMING, I stopped him.

"Alright. This is one of those words where you drop the last letter, silent *E*, before adding -ING. Exactly the same way as we did long ago with HAPPY and HAPPILY. We did not hear the *Y* in that, but we had to change it before adding our ending. We do not hear the *E* in COME." He brightened. He remembered our long ago tenet.

"C-O-M-ing?"

"Yes. C-O-M-ing." He went on writing.

He looked up again when he came to LEARNED. He knew this, too, was probably a bit tricky.

"It is the root word LE*A*RN, with another silent A thrown in right in the middle. Visualize it in your mind. These silent vowels we do not hear are killers, Roy. I agree." He nodded and smiled.

"L-E-A-R-N?" he asked, after staring into space to see the word in his mind's eye.

"Yes. With -ED as the ending." He wrote it correctly after first spelling it out loud to himself. Our myriad conversations about endings were paying off, big time.

At the word GETTING, I merely stated, "With this word, we double the T before adding -ING." He got it beautifully, not even bothering to pronounce the word out loud first to himself. He wrote GETTING after first looking up into thin air to "see" the word. At SMARTER, he hesitated.

"It's the SM sound, plus the word ART," I offered, "kind of like START, which we covered a few lessons back. With SMARTER, you add yet another ending, this time it is -ER. Smart-ER. SMARTER," I repeated to emphasize the new -ER ending. He thought just a minute.

"S-M-A-R-T-E-R?" I merely nodded as he went on to write the word correctly, looking pleased with himself.

We continued in this turtle-like mode, sounding out words and endings innumerable times along the way: Starting and stopping, starting and stopping, much as we had done in the Walt Disney story — until we finally came to the end of the letter.

"Before you write LOVE, ROY, which is called the Closing, you need to drop down one line and begin writing way over here." I pointed to a spot two-thirds of the way across the page.

"Over here?" he again asked, askance.

"You got it. Now, please write LOVE with a capital letter, followed by another comma, and all on the same line. This closure is much like your opening greeting or salutation: You must use a comma." No problem, he wrote both.

"Drop down another line to sign the letter, and write ROY almost directly under LOVE." He finished and looked up, expecting more.

"That's it, Friend. You have just written your first letter."

"Boy howdy. That don't seem like much — now," and he turned to grin at me over his glasses.

"Before you take those glasses off, I want you please to read your letter back to me in its entirety." He looked puzzled, but complied. What I wanted Roy Caddell to hear was the tone of his own voice as he read. His inflection was gradually improving. He no longer sounded like a first grader when he read. But, he did not sound like a graduate yet, either. He began anew. As he finished, he turned to me, utterly amazed.

"Well. What do you think?" I excitedly asked.

"We done good here. I cain't hardt-ly believe I done wrote a letter. Wait 'til I tell Hazel. I know I needt practice writin' like this, and I wanna be doin' more of it. This here is somethin'."

"So are you, Sir. It wasn't so bad after all, now was it, Mr. Caddell?" I asked teasingly.

"Trude. I learnt a long time ago that you don't never ask me 'ta do nuthin' that ain't f'r my own good. Now I'm real gladt we done this today, I shore am." So was I.

This was to be this man's first letter, but not his last. Hanging on the wall by my wrapping closet is one of the cleverest letters I have ever received — framed, from this gentleman. Two years hence, Roy Caddell was to tell me that he had written his very first birthday card to his Mother.

We had scaled high mountains on this day.

Three words terribly misused, all but butchered by our populace in written form, are TO, TOO and TWO. These three tiny words continually cropped up in our conversations. Roy Caddell did not know there was a difference among them. To him, they represented one word.

When I first presented these words on paper to him this day, he immediately recognized TWO. But TO and TOO were a complete enigma. I handed him the three written on a single word card and asked him to read them back to me. He merely shook his head. He looked first at the words and then at me, blank. Nothing.

It was as if he could not believe I was telling him, *let alone showing him*, that there are *three* twos, with three separate meanings. The very audacity! Had I not been looking at him in earnest, he would have thought I was teasing. My eyes told him otherwise.

Finally, he slowly said, "Well. I know this one's a writin' two 'n this one's a money two. The money two I know, Trude. But them other two? I don't have no i-dear." So we began again.

"All right, Friend. All three of these words sound alike and are pronounced exactly the same. That is the easy part. It is only usage and spelling that are hard. The everyday use of these three words in written form is what throws most people. I do not want them to throw you. Thus, I bring my latest offering," I wryly commented.

"I a-presheate that. I real-ly do. If you think I need'ta know somethin', then I wanna learn it. But these three words? Trude, them's not so friendt-ly. Some a them words I don't like so much. These look like they're gonna be some a them. . . .

"Why do *they* try 'n make all this hard, like this here? Why don't *they* just use two a them twos?"

"Oh, Roy," I laughed, "you ask the greatest questions! I do not know the answer, you know that. I only know there are three of these cute little devils, and they like you even if you don't like them. They are not at all discriminatory, like some people I know. . . ." It was his turn to laugh. He knew he'd been "had." I continued.

"This first TO is really a preposition, and the words that come after it form what is called a 'prepositional phrase.' We have talked about this at least once before, the day we were making our sentences. You said that day, 'The cattle are *in the barn.*' I told you then that 'in the barn' is a prepositional phrase."

"Seems like I r'member somethin' like that," he mused.

"Yes. I rather thought you would. Anyone who can remember linking verbs I casually mentioned that same day, and then reel them off to me days later, I know is remembering about ninety percent of what I'm throwing out.

"In fact, Sir, I have not found one thing you have forgotten, that we have worked through and learned together. My solid opinion is that these three little words will be a cakewalk for you." He beamed.

"An example of the word TO," and I continued as I spelled the word out as I wrote it on his yellow pad, is, "I am going TO town." In that particular sentence, you use the one spelled T-O. TO town. TO get Hazel. TO feed the cows. TO run get gas. TO the grocery. TO class. TO the library." He did not move.

"This second TOO is the one I like, and the one I use most often. But, it is also the hardest of the three and the one most misused.

"T-O-O," and I spelled it out as I wrote it, "simply means 'also,' or 'in addition to,' as in the sentence, 'I am going TO town, TOO.'"

"As in," and I shifted the pitch of my voice, "Wait for me. I want TO go with you, TOO." He laughed, then quickly realized what I was saying.

"That's it? That's the dif'rence in them other two words? One of 'em's somethin' 'bout distance,

"Sinc'dt I knowt there's a diff'rence now, I care that I learn 'em right. Then, I can use 'em where I want 'ta. But, I shore din't like 'em none when I first saw 'em. They was badt."

like, over there? And that other one I shore don't much like, but I know I gotta have. . . ." His words trailed off in disbelief. Surely, this was a ruse.

"That's it. Most people use that first TO and completely forget about that other tiny TOO with the extra O tacked onto the end. Yes, sir. That is it."

"Well, I'll be. Surely I can r'member that little bit. I figure if we keep this up f'r fifteen years, I'll learn all you're a tryin'ta teach me. You know, since I been savin' mosta my brain all these years, there ain't no tellin' how smart I'd real-ly be if I couldt r'member all you're teachin' me.

"Act-ually, this here is makin' an awful lotta sense 'ta me. And the funny part is, I like doin' this stuff. I shore hadn't plann'dt on enjoyin' it so much. Each time's as good or better than the last.

"Maybe that's why so many a them other people like me drop outta this learnin'ta read 'n write. They forgit to have them some fun along the way." He sat smiling and pondering.

Quite honestly, he scarcely could believe he would *think* such a thing, let alone say it. He watched me grinning as I wrote his words down as fast as I could. He read my mind.

"Trude. I ain't never talk'dt this much in my whole life. One a these days, I'm gonna come here 'n I ain't sayin' nuthin'. I'm just gonna sit."

"Sir. Have you ever heard of *fat chance* on either of us doing that?" His grin encompassed the room.

Yep. He "shore" was right. It did not take TOO much TO make the TWO of us happy. Particularly, when one of us kept asking the other one which *two* they were continually using conversationally in sentences. There were times that the man must have felt like I was a recurring nightmare. Scary.

For every risk I took with Roy Caddell, there were tremendous rewards. He bloomed like a flower. I was but a vehicle in his ardent search for knowledge. He literally was starved for education and conversation. I but fed his insatiable appetite.

Slowly but surely, he began to feel better about himself, to walk taller, to nod that white hat of his toward others, even to smile on occasion. *Simply because he could read!* Maybe not everything, but *something!* And for someone like Roy, something can be everything, and is most definitely better that nothing.

The man was changing. Originally, he did not like it. But now? "Now" was another world and he liked what he was becoming. He was feeding his mind while nourishing his soul. He did not know he had been so thirsty.

Roy Caddell was developing much needed self-confidence and pride, simply because he took a chance, — on himself, on someone else.

This was his Journey of a Lifetime. Not only had we caught the correct train, we were headed down the right track, riding in the first-class compartment. The man deserved it.

THE ULTIMATE SCARLET LETTER

*"Well now, Trude, anytime they'd ask me what my
address was, I'd pretendt I din't hear 'em. Then, I'd
ask'ta take their paper outta my truck, or home w'th
me 'ta fill it out there, if they'd let me. 'Cause I'd
knowt I couldtn't write nuthin' out there in front a
nobody. They'da knowt f'r shore that I couldn't readt
'n write,'n I couldn't have that. T'weren't nuthin' I
couldt do 'bout it but keep on the way I was goin'."*

Roy Caddell did not know his complete address. I was horrified!
Horrified that I never even had suspected. Horrified that my texts had
not alerted me to this possibility. I had not considered, even for a
moment, that he might not know his address. "Elementary, my dear
Watson. Elementary." I flunked.

Realization came to me slowly. I simply had a feeling, although I will
admit, it took me some time to "put my finger on it." Probably because
I never had done this. Probably because, initially, Roy could read some
things. Probably because he was a good bluffer.

But suddenly, I knew, and I felt like warmed-over death. It was the
only time I can ever recall wanting to run — far, far away.

Why was this not mentioned right up front in my adult instruction
books? In tutor training classes? In the very first lessons of the tutor
handbook?

This was something my friend absolutely *had to know*. This we could
not skirt. I was aghast, appalled. I felt violated. I had made the mistak-
en assumption that, of course, Roy Caddell knew his own address.
Orally, written, I'd take it in whatever primitive form it came.

Never one time had I thought to confront this. It would have been
so easy, particularly in that early lesson where we covered the spelling

of ADDRESS. *That* would have been the logical time for him to learn his. I chided myself for not having once thought of it. How foolish of me. How selfish.

One day in June, in Lesson Ten, my text made mention that "the names in a phone book are in alphabetical order." Roy knew this, but some small glimmer in his eyes that day suddenly clicked for me — and I knew. "Oh, Trude. How could you have missed *this?*" The degradation he must have suffered pained me to the point of nausea. So, I flat out asked him, afraid of the answer.

"Roy, do you know your address?"

"Uh. No. Not all of it." He sheepishly grinned, and looked embarrassed.

"Roy! You *have* to know your own address! What part do you know, and what part not?" I distinctly remember I raised my voice to him in abject horror.

"Well now, Trude . . ." he began in his own defense.

"There is no 'Well' to it, Roy. Not knowing your address will give you away. *Every single time!* No exceptions. We *have* to learn this." He immediately knew, from the consternation in my voice, that *this* was serious. Serious? This was base degradation! This was rape.

So, he told me, in a low voice as he stared the table down, not once turning my way. He had known that, eventually, I would catch this flaw. He simply did not expect such a severe reprisal.

"I knowt my box number. I'm pret-ty shore it's 8-6-4. I've practic'dt it a bunch so's I couldt make shore I couldt write it right when I need'dt it."

"And your zip code?"

"Uh. No. That's the part I ain't never learnt — yet."

So it was true. It was as though he were homeless. I felt dumber than a post. I slumped in my seat as he continued, my stomach feeling like the middle had just been chopped out.

"Anytime they'd ask me what my address was, I'd pretendt I din't hear 'em. Then, I'd ask'ta take their paper outta my truck, or home w'th me 'ta fill it out there, if they'dt let me. 'Cause I'd knowt I couldtn't write nuthin' out there in front a nobody. They'da knowt f'r shore I couldn't read 'n write. I couldn't have that." He was staring ahead.

"So's, I hadt me a little scrap a paper in my bill-fold't that hadt all that im-port'nt stuff wrote down on. I'd go outside't 'n pull that paper out 'n copy off whatever it was I need'dt. Then I'd go back in and return their paper to 'em, if they'd let me." Finally, he turned my way. He looked sad.

"For years, I did that, Trude. I din't go *nowheres* w'thout that slip a paper. I carried it w'th me 'til I wore it out. Then I made't me up another one. I might even still have it somewheres here in my bill-fold. . . ." But he did not. I thought I was going to be physically ill. Fortunately, he went on.

"Or, if it was a job app-li-ca-shun, I'd just tell 'em I'd bring their paper back to 'em the next day, that I'd forgot'ta pack my glasses — somethin' like that. I al-ways made't me up some x'cus'dt. I use 'ta do that all the time. That there was just a way a life f'r me back then. T'weren't nuthin' I couldt do 'bout it but keep on the way I was goin'."

I sat in stony silence, unable to believe this conver-sation. My throat felt like the hangman had already been there. My face must have been chalky white, Roy could tell I was shaken.

"That's what I been tellin' you, Trude. But you *cannot* understandt it. There ain't no ways you can ever knowt what it's like not'ta be able'ta read 'n write. T'ain't no way." His body was still as he stared into space, his hands clasped in front of him, his head bowed. Finally, he turned to me with sor-rowful eyes.

"Bein' married't has han-dicapp'dt me in another sense't there, too." I looked up, genuinely surprised and puzzled.

"I mean that. When I was single, I *had'ta* learn 'ta do them things f'r myself. Like that scrap a paper. I had'ta haf me some little somethin' 'ta help me. *I couldt not do it alone!*

"When I was married't, I let my wife do them things f'r me. That was bad, *f'r me*. I shouldn't haf done it, but I did. I shouldt a kept doin' them things f'r myself. I'da been lots betters off."

His impassioned pleas were capsulated. His coursing words let me know he desperately needed me to follow his lonely line of thinking. The words I could grasp — but, the roads he had traveled? Never. My mind was racing as I sought to find my voice. It had been hiding behind a silent sobbing gasp. Suddenly, I thought of an analogy.

"You paint a perfect picture of two marvelous words I dearly love, Roy. *Empathy* and *sympathy*. Empathy means that you have been there, it has happened to you. Sympathy means you have deep feeling for someone. You are sympathetic with their tragedy or pain, but you have not experienced it yourself.

"You are right. I cannot empathize with you, not one bit. I have not walked in your shoes, I never will. But, Sir, I sympathize with you more than I can ever verbalize to you. My very soul hurts for you, Roy Caddell. You are my dear, dear friend."

He pondered my explanation but a moment, then noticeably relaxed. Finally, he quietly spoke.

"It's true. I been hurt a bunch in my life. But sinc't I been comin' down here 'n talkin'ta you, I learnt *ever'*body's been hurt, one way or the other. I'm luckier than most, I gots you to help me. And Hazel. I *am* one a the lucky ones." He looked up and softly smiled.

"Now. About them two wordts. I hearda that Sym-parthy. I just never knowt how'ta use it befor' now. No one ever toldt me what it meant, 'n I shore never ask'dt.

"Trude, one thing about it: You come closer than anyone I ever know'ta understandin' all this. But you're right. You ain't never gonna be able'ta do that em-paRthy with me. But, you try, real hardt." He brightly smiled for the first time all day.

"That is only because you talk to me, Mr. Caddell. And for that, I shall be eternally grateful."

"That's 'cause you're easy to talk to, you listen real goodt. I like talkin'ta you, 'n I don't 'x-actly understandt that neither. I don't talk to many people, Trude. 'Specially not women!" He smiled wistfully at himself, as I laughed uproariously. Once again, we began.

First, I told him that those clever tricks he confessed to, and used, were dead give-aways, like forgetting his glasses. Red-flag warning. Fire alarm. People know, or they guess, if it happens very often. They simply choose to say nothing.

This startled him. He had thought *these* were the perfect excuses. After all, this was his way of life, most people he associated with used these same ploys. Ploys which were, in actuality, only thinly veiled disguises.

Sadly, these excuses had become permanent roadblocks for my friend. He had so focused a lifetime of fear into shutting out and saving face, that he had never considered his position from the other side of the fence. This was Roy Caddell's solitary mirror: A distorted reflection, with no depth and no hope. He was entrapped in his own reasoning.

This was the "catch 22" in which I continually found myself. Every tutor does. Desperately trying to *teach* this man while struggling to *reach* this man, his inner soul. No wonder it took us so long.

Roy Caddell certainly learned his address and zip code. About this, he knew I would be unmercifully tenacious, unrelenting. He knew he desperately *needed* this knowledge. He mastered both quickly because he practiced, over and over and over again — so no one would suspect his terrible secret. His initial method was simplistic, but absolutely powerful.

Our next session, I happened to glance his way as we sat down to work. There, on his left wrist, were his address and zip code, primitively printed. In ink! And there they stayed, until they finally wore off — I know not when.

To this day, whenever I receive a letter from him with his return address beautifully written out in full, in the upper left-hand corner of the envelope, I think of that ink so deftly hidden under his sleeve. His safeguard from outside danger, and from me.

It shall ever remain the indelible stain on my heart.

Dictionaries were an omnipresent topic in class sessions. If we were not using Roy's, we were flying out the door to use the gigantic one on the second floor. The library staff was accustomed to seeing us dart back and forth between our room and their bookstand. My friend originally did not like it.

In fairness, a dictionary was not of his world. I respected that. Dictionaries were of my world. He respected that. It always shocked me to see how lost he was in that marvelous book, how long it took him to find a word — any word.

Slowly, however, the book became a friend to this man. His initial negative reaction shifted into neutral. His world was broadening. His once safe concrete hull had a crack in it, and I did not tell him.

What I did tell Roy Caddell, in labyrinthine conversations, was that I grew up in a home where education and knowledge were highly stressed. These, along with honor, integrity and your good name, reigned supreme.

College graduations were times of celebration within my family, especially for my grandfather.

He did not have a degree. His came from the "School of Hard Knocks," which was also highly respected. There was certainly nothing wrong with "hands-on experience."

Oddly enough, Roy seemed to thrive on these familial tales. He relished hearing them.

"You real-ly get into all this stuff, don't you?" he observed as he shook his head in amazement one day. "I *cannot* imagine your spendin' all the time you do on this, f'r someone you hardt-ly knowt. I just ain't never met nobody like you."

"Yes, I guess I do. This speaks to my very soul, Roy. What I am desperately trying to teach you is of paramount importance to me, *for you*. It is the difference between life and living."

"I can tell that. Boy howdy."

I went on to relate how two of my junior high English teachers, Mrs. Wiest and Mrs. Norris, drilled language into me. They were tough sergeants, who put up with little guff from students. I did well in their classes because I loved what they taught. I learned my grammar from pros, both at home and at school.

"Learning is always with me, Roy. It is an integral part of who I am. But, if you think I am *into all this*, you should see my mother. She is a fanatic when it comes to learning and broadening her mind, her horizons. Far and away, she and my entire family are the most inquisitively intellectual people I have ever been around."

"Then she must be like you," he offered, "'cause you're the most in-tel-lectual person I've ever been aroundt."

"Oh, no, it's not even a close vote. I am like my mother in many ways, but I will never be at her level intellectually. Through my growing up years, and even today, lovingly she will correct my grammar. It is an ongoing saga. By now, Sir," I said grinning, "you know I need lots of help."

He sat with chin in hand and a smile on his face, raptly listening and trying to imagine such a household.

He could not.

"I GIT A LITTLE MORE LOVE F'R THE DICTSHUNARY EVER' DAY. NOW, I THINK IT WOULDT BE FUN 'TA SIT DOWN 'N GO THRU THERE 'N LEARN ALL THEM WORDTS. ONCE'T YA GIT 'TA THE OTHER SID'T A THE RIVER WHEN THERE WEREN'T NO BRIDGE THERE BEFOR', YA REALLY DONE SOMETHIN'."

"As dictionaries go, Mr. Caddell, my parents have the same one as the library has outside. My grandfather gave it to them three Christmases ago. It sits on an antique book stand in their home, where it is used *every single day.* My mother considers that book as vital to her life as food or water, shelter or love. The dictionary is nourishment for her soul."

"So," he queried, "that is where you get all y'ur excitement f'r this, from y'ur mother." It was more a statement that a question.

"Yes. From my mother, from my family. Certainly from my grandfather who, throughout his entire life, anytime he did not know something, would head to the nearest public library to find answers.

"We are *all* vitally interested in learning, and in growing as human beings. We constantly push ourselves to absorb new thoughts and concepts.

"Now do you see why I push you so hard at times? I want you to know another world that is out there, Roy — a world to which you and I will never travel, *except through books and learning!*

"I have tried to pass these same inquisitive qualities on to my two children. Constantly, I send them newspaper clippings, even more than what I continually bring to class for you. Truly, Mr. Caddell, I am not picking on you."

He smiled, knowing full well my adult children must receive thick packets weekly from a mother off on another tangent. He was not far off.

Nowhere in my Laubach teaching materials did I find mention of a dictionary as being an appropriate tool for beginning readers. Not in the first workbook, not in the second, and not yet in the third. I would have to disagree with that thinking and approach, particularly with adult beginning readers.

It appears to me there is no logic to such thinking, no pattern for basis. These people are not brain-dead, they are only brain-starved.

It could be interpreted that, by not teaching nonreaders how to use a dictionary, it is an *intended silent slur*. If adults care enough to come to learn to read and write, they care enough to learn. Period. That includes dictionaries.

The one negative to any dictionary usage is *getting started*. It takes time. The concept is not embraced by students immediately. But, which one is in this convoluted educational learning process?

Roy Caddell is a viable *literacy yardstick,* representing perhaps countless millions. He is exactly what the literacy movement is all about. *He* is the one we tutors strive to reach.

He benefitted from a dictionary, albeit reluctantly, when we started using one on our third day of lessons. We have not yet stopped. This man's appetite for knowledge is insatiable. I but fed his hunger, with a book chock-full of answers to every imaginable question.

Granted, at one time, Roy wanted to throw his dictionary in the trash. Now, he would go find another. Initially, our battle over a dictionary was a Mexican standoff: He waited for me to *tell* him to retrieve his; I waited for him to find words.

Originally, Mr. Caddell thought he could outwait me. He found out he was mistaken. I have the patience of Job on many things. This was one battle he lost. He never really stood a chance.

If you have any doubts on the subject of dictionaries, go ask him. Do not take my word for it. The man will tell you himself, in no uncertain terms. Just be prepared for an onslaught, he does not mince words.

Today, four years hence, we meet weekly in a small second floor room, where our own private *large* dictionary awaits us. It is a much used, out-of-date model that is now out of circulation, but one which the library staff has kindly provided for our usage. We are most grateful.

Roy considers this merely "showin' proper respect." Some things never change.

AUTO MECHANICS AND WORD MECHANICS

*"Practicin' them letters 'n then writin' them words
down stokes my brain. Maybe if it gets real hot in
there, the right thing might pop out!"*

How we got off on this tangent, I never have been quite sure. Maybe Roy picked up on these words in conversation, as I was talking about various aspects of our language. Maybe I heard him try to use them correctly in his speech. Maybe he thought he could master these. I shall never quite know how all this began. . . .

Whatever, the end product was both brilliant and startling. The end result was Roy Caddell's "Big Word List," which produced some of the most hilarious class sessions encountered. True, he would not use these words in public — but, oh, the sentences he came up with in class, the pronunciations. We often rolled with laughter.

The man has a razor-sharp sense of humor. He is one of the funniest people I have ever known in my entire life. Unintentionally. Wit is but one of his God-given talents. Laughter is one of ours.

Before I could even get the question of homework out of my mouth this day, Roy addressed the assignment himself.

"I din't get much done at home, but this. All them words written down you ever give me. I couldn't 'x-actly r'member what it was you toldt me 'ta do, so I just wrote 'em all down." I nearly fell out of my chair.

"This" consumed three entire pages of his legal tablet. The second sheet was divided into three columns, or 38 lines times 3: 114 words on that one page alone! I could scarcely believe my eyes. This laborious effort had taken mounds of time and would aid him in every arena.

Talk about beautiful penmanship, the man had it. He writes so anyone can read it. His cursive letters are gorgeous, his words totally legible, an unbeatable combination. Roy Caddell had come a long way since that first day, because he worked at it. His secret and shame were safe in the handwriting department.

"Trude, if nothin' else, writin' down these words'll help me w'th my spellin'. If I keep on like this, I figure I'll end up learnin' how'ta spell 'em. Practicin' them letters 'n then writin' down them words stokes my brain. Maybe if it gets real hot in there, the right thing might pop out!" His face softened as he watched me laugh uncontrollably.

Amongst the reams of writing presented today were the humongous words COMPREHENSION, CONVERSATION, CONNOTATION, COMMUNICATION, ABBREVIATION and VETERINARIAN.

Never would I have selected these for spelling exercises, had I been doing the choosing. I was not. This complex group of words was *his choice*, he had singled them out. I had not assigned them. His reasoning was simple. . .

"These are the words I needt help learnin' how'ta spell. *Not them little ones.* 'Special-ly sinc't I pret-ty near know how'ta spell all a them. The big words is what I need'ta work on. *This* here is 'x-actly what I needt right now."

"Fine by me, Friend. But, I want you to know that we start with the very hardest words you have written. Hardest in that these are the longest to spell. But, they really do spell pretty much like they sound. We can do this, it will simply take time."

"That's all I got, Trude. Time."

While these six seemingly complex words look as if they are far beyond the scope of this man's abilities at this point in time, they were not. He was familiar with each from class conversations. Not one word ever appeared on his "Big Word" list that he did not know the meaning. Not one entry was taken directly from dictionary wording. Not one entry was logged after we had looked up a given word and its meaning in a dictionary. What he wrote opposite each term was strictly his wordage: What came to his mind and "popped" out was what I wrote down, laughing all the way.

Quite honestly, I believe Roy Caddell endorsed these words because these were the very ones he had spent his whole life avoiding, like the bubonic plague. Given his background, perhaps these would be the very ones *I* most would have wanted to learn, had I been in his position. I cannot say.

His complete "Big Word List" is reproduced at the back of this book. Enjoy. It warms my heart every time I read it. It would warm the heart of a rock.

Although he embraced these complex words, what Roy did not know was how to spell them, our job today. All endeavors for reading and writing eventually led back to basic spelling.

In my opinion, the only way to teach reading is to teach spelling *at the exact same time*. This man's constant concerns about spelling were on target. I was just trying to break his fears down into manageable increments.

"See where you have written 'Reading Compre<u>c</u>hension?'" I asked, pointing to the word near the top of the page.

"Ahh. Yes."

"First, I will say the word correctly, then sound it out by syllables. *Listen* for the letter sounds here, Roy. Then, I want you to spell this word again on your paper. You will see for yourself why that "C" I underlined does not belong in there. Now, watch my mouth carefully."

Slowly, I enunciated COMPREHENSION several times, first as the whole word, and then in its syllabic parts — pointing to the page as we worked. He watched closely, then laboriously repeated it. It was another tricky R word. For Roy, these were difficult.

"All right. Let's begin again. I want you to see *why* and *how* some of these are misspelled." I picked up his tablet from his direct line of vision and tore out a sheet of paper for him to work on. He knew what was coming, we'd been here before.

"IF I HAD'TA MAKE A CHOICE 'TWEEN READIN' 'N SPELLIN', I'DT CHOOSE THE READIN' EVER' TIME. I CAN READT TWO 'TA ONE OV'R THE SPELLIN'. BUT I KNOWT NOW, THAT YA CAIN'T READT PROPERLY W'THOUT BOTH THE WRITIN' 'N THE SPELLIN'. I GOTS ME A WAYS 'TA GO ON SPELLIN'."

From similar exercises, he had realized immediate and beneficial results, which was why we were here.

"Now, I want you to spell only the first syllable right now. Listen for the sounds of the letters. COM," I slowly started.

"C-O-M?" he queried. I nodded as he wrote.

"PRE. ComPREhension. PRE. R<u>E</u>. R<u>E</u>," I stressed.

"P-E? R-A?"

"The first one was close. You are leaving out a letter, that you said the second time. Watch my mouth closely. PRE. Rrrr. PRE. ComPREEEEhension. Just like it sounds, Roy. Comp<u>re</u>hension."

"RE?" he asked dubiously.

"Yes. E. It is called a long E, you hear the letter say itself. ComPREhension." He slowly wrote P-R-E connected to C-O-M. He turned for further instructions as he finished.

"HEN. Like a chicken hen. CompreHENsion. HEN."

"Hen . . ." he started to ask, but answered before he could get the question fully out of his mouth. "HEN." It was a flat statement of fact. We were three-fourths of the way there.

"OK, Roy. These last four letters sound like the letters S-H-U-N. But, they are not. The letters you will write here are S-I-O-N. In our complex English language, the SHUN sound is written several ways: T-I-O-N, S-I-O-N, I-O-N and I-A-N. Each is pronounced generally the same way: SHUN. We use the S-I-O-N version with COMPREHEN<u>SION</u>." He slowly finished writing the word. C-O-M-P-R-E-H-E-N-S-I-O-N was before him.

"Now, Sir. Do you see why I could look at that word as you had originally written it and ascertain there was no C in there?"

"Ahh. Yes. This here just looks better, more right. Now."

"Exactly. It *looks* right. With that extra C thrown in, it did not *look* right to me. Once again, Roy, I'm coming in the Back Door on spelling. If a word does not look right to me, I check its spelling in my dictionary — or, run the risk of its being wrong.

"Now. I want you to see something else. Please write this same word with the letters S-H-U-N on the end, instead of the correct S-I-O-N ending." He dutifully wrote COMPREHEN<u>SHUN</u>.

"Nope." he stated as he had no more than finished writing. "It don't look right spell'dt this way. Hmph. I'll be. This other way looks right."

"Exactly. It *looks* right. Be patient with yourself, Roy. Correct spelling will come. You did not get into this fix overnight. You will not correct all your maladies overnight either. You *will* learn how to spell."

"I hear you. It shore seems easy when you break it down like this. Still 'n all, COMPREHENSION is a might-ty big word, Trude."

"It is. We are agreed. But, it's not quite as big as it was, is it. . . ?" He grinned and nodded in the negative.

"OK. Now, we are going to take COMPREHENSION and break it down again. Do not write anything here, please listen. I believe you will *hear* each syllable become a more easily managed part you can better pronounce." I clapped out the four syllables as I repeated them in cadence: "COM-PRE-HEN-SION. COM-PRE-HEN-SION. COMPREHENSION."

"Com-Pre-Hen-Sion," he slowly repeated.

"Again."

"Com-Pree-Hen-Shun."

"Again."

"Comprehen-shun."

"Again."

We repeated the process in sing-song fashion, for emphasis. I wanted this syllable breakdown embedded in this man's mind.

"Now, Roy. Look at your paper and put a line under each syllable that we have repeated, and *that you hear* in COMPREHENSION."

He underlined the four divisions exactly. <u>COM</u>-<u>PRE</u>-<u>HEN</u>-<u>SION</u> stood out on his paper. He cast a sideways glance at me to see how he was doing. I was beaming. So was he.

"Now. Remember what we have learned about vowels and have gone over repeatedly: For every syllable, there is at least one vowel sound; in every syllable, there is at least one vowel. What are those marvelously friendly critters?"

"Ahh. A, E, I, O . . . U, and sometimes that W and Y."

"Perfect. Now please go back to the four syllables you just underlined, and put another little line under the vowel in each. Use my heavy black pen so your marks will stand out." He went straight to work and correctly double underlined every vowel he found. He did not miss one! He looked up to survey the dissected word before him.

"Well, I'll be. C<u>o</u>m-pr<u>e</u>-h<u>e</u>n-s<u>i</u>on. Comprehension," he softly repeated, in awe of himself and his sizeable accomplishment. He slowly turned his face to mine, gratitude shone forth.

"Trude, I am gettin' good outta this. Maybe now I can spell them other wordts. . . ." His voice trailed off as he shook his head in disbelief.

"Or," I offered, "you will be able to get far enough into a word you are spelling, by sounding out the letters, to either reach for your dictionary or write the word on paper — then go from there. I think we are on the right track, Roy. But, what do you think?"

"I know we are. But, y'ur shore makin' it soundt pret-ty easy doin' it this way. I like it."

"Well. Some words are fairly easy to spell. Some are not, they are killers. Always focus on the easy ones, Roy, and remember: These words are trying to help you, with their individual letters and sounds. Please try and like them." I looked his way wistfully.

Already, in thirty short minutes, we had made powerful strides. I, of course, had prepared a lesson, but it was obvious we would never get to it. Oftentimes our lessons seemed to follow a course of their own. We but navigated the flow, within parameters.

My only concern was that I honor my promise that we finish this first workbook soon. We were behind schedule, but definitely making heavy-duty progress. He all but read my mind.

"It's like I toldt my wife this mornin', if somethin' ever was to happen, and we didn't get no more done than this here, this first workbook has help'dt me a bunch. I feel like I've learnt so much I real-ly need'dta know, things I miss'dt.

"Befor', I *couldt'nt* read 'n write, Trude. I wouldn't ever try'ta do any a this. I shore wouldt never a tried'ta spell them words. I wouldtn't never even *try*'ta learn. Now, I'd at least haf'ta try.

"The reason I never want'dta learn'ta read 'n write befor' is 'cause *I couldt not do it myself.* No ways. I had'ta have me some help. And now? I do not quite understand it myself why I enjoy this so much, but I real-ly do. Now, I wanna learn all I can."

"Am I glad to hear that, Sir. I thought you were getting ready to tell me you were not coming back to class. Make no mistake about it, Roy Caddell, I would come after you — with a vengeance. I will do whatever it takes, and drive wherever I have to go, for you to learn to read and write."

"No, no! This here takes top priority aroundt our house. Top bjllin'. It comes first, right after my family 'n my work w'th them cows."

"The cows and I thank you for that vote of confidence, Sir! I thought I might be in real trouble, but it looks like you are going to keep both the cows *and* me. Lucky us." We both were laughing as we prepared to delve further into the harder words he had brought with him.

Again, we began tearing apart and rebuilding words. Others needed our immediate attention before we could go home. We proceeded slowly, mechanically. It took us over two hours to break down eight or ten words, and the various derivatives easily spotted within each.

Roy did not care how we went about the words on his paper. He only cared that we do them — today. He was rather like Brer Rabbit in that ole briar patch. *"Throw me in again. . . ."* I obliged him.

The one thing I did before going further, was to write the four word endings for SHUN at the top of his legal sheet. Beside each, I wrote an equal sign, then the letters -SHUN. Although they sounded identical, for the most part, each was spelled differently. I wanted to give him every advantage.

Thus, his paper looked like this: -TION = -SHUN; -SION = -SHUN; -ION = -SHUN; -IAN = -SHUN

These new endings, I told Roy, he simply must memorize and become familiar with because, from here on out, he was going to run across words spelled with each. He already had and, of course, he had not known why.

"These four endings are little different than -ED, -ING, -LY. All endings are added onto root words, the word as it is presented without endings. That is where this starts, Roy: The original word, standing alone. We always get back to Square One.

"The trick for you, is that you see these bigger words and immediately think you cannot spell them. That is not true. Look for endings and then back up — see what is left, the root word. Then try and spell that, by sounding out first the letters, then the word. I think you will do better with that approach.

"Please stop telling yourself you cannot spell. That is not true. You might not be able to spell many words, but neither can I. The reverse also holds true: There are many words that we can spell. Let's focus on the positive and go from there, Mr. Caddell." I smiled as he brightened.

We always came back to the same seven and six: If I did not take it upon myself to explain a rule or reason why, he would not know. He would not ask, and he could not guess the correlation in this maze at this stage of the game.

With few exceptions, the man had "seen 'em that way lottsa times, but I shore never knowt why." He had spent his adult life on the outside, looking in — without once being invited into the party. It saddened me.

While we had not yet ventured into long vowel pronunciation, as we worked our way through lessons, their inclusion was unavoidable. They were obvious, we had talked of these several times. Long vowels are friendly, long vowels you can hear and see, almost touch. He would like these in the third workbook.

We also had skirted the concept that countless words are spelled one logical way, yet enunciated entirely differently from what their spellings indicate. Our language is full of such complex words.

These were all confusing concepts for Roy Caddell, but ones which he *knew* he had to have. After all, such oddities in our language were here to stay. He *had* to absorb them at some time. Now seemed as good a time as any.

"Them's not friendt-ly, Trude. Some words aren't never pronounc'dt like the'r spell'dt. *That's the hard part for me.* I'm tryin'ta make room f'r this here, it just takes some gettin' us'dta."

"Agreed, this is the hard part. But, if it's any consolation to you, that is the hard part for everyone. How many times have you watched me try to spell, and flunk. Sometimes I'm so far off base, I have to go outside for help." He smiled weakly as we continued.

The next word we tackled was CONNOTATION. I pointed out the small word NOT, and asked him to find another word tucked inside this big word. He found NO.

"That was what I had hoped you would find, Roy. That is how the word is pronounced: You hear the word NO inside, with emphasis on the long O. OOOOO. CON<u>NO</u>TATION. CONNOTATION." Again, we worked through the word. This one went faster.

"Roy, let me give you two ways this word CONNOTATION is trying to be friendly:

One. If we take the first part of the word and change one tiny letter, the first O to an A, we have the word CANNOT.

Two. If we take the last six letters of the word and mentally place the letter S before them, we have the word STATION."

I placed my hands over both parts of the word so he could see only the applicable letters for each of the "new" words. He was studying the paper, and the one big word, CONNOTATION.

"Try and see these in your mind's eye, Roy. Then write both on your paper and see what I mean. We will take them one at a time." He sat staring into space. He slowly began writing, softly talking to himself.

"A in place a that O. A f'r O. . . ." CANNOT clearly appeared before him. He turned, genuinely surprised.

"CANNOT," he mused as he surveyed his work. "Hrmph. I'da shore never knowt it was spell'dt as one word. If I'da seen it that way befor' today, I'da thought it was wrong.

"Trude. I can probab-ly r'member CANNOT. But I won't never use it outsid'a here. If I ever need that word, I'd use a little ole farm word. Ain't nobody out by me ever gonna know what CANNOT means anyways." I dissolved into laughter. Touché.

"Now," I said, covering the first part of CONNOTATION, "tell me what we would have if you put that S before these remaining six letters?" I waited patiently while he again stared into space. This was a word we had never even spoken of, never mentioned. This was cold turkey. I wanted this man to see how easy some spelling can be.

I kept repeating CONNOTATION with the emphasis on the last two syllables. "ConnoTATION. CONNO<u>TATION</u>. Conno-tation. Add the S, Roy. What do you have?"

"STA . . . Sta-shun?" he asked, in a most startled tone.

"Station," I concurred emphatically. "The word STATION. S-T-A-T-I-O-N. Now write it on your paper."

"Well, I'll be. I cain't hardt-ly believe I can spell a word like this. I just haf'ta learn'ta myself, I can do this. Wait 'til I go home and tell 'em!"

"Of course you can do this. All we have done is to break these words apart and put them back together again. Or, to tear them down and substitute another letter, before putting the word back together."

"You do the same things with a car as you tear up the motor. You take out that motor, work on it, perhaps substitute some parts, then put the whole rebuilt motor back where it belongs — together again.

"We do the same thing here, Roy, only in another venue. Break down, build back. Break down, build back."

"But it shore sounds different when you do it this way. . . ."

"Yes, it surely does. But, so do your car motors when they run correctly. *I* can generally *hear* and *see* the difference in words if they are not as they are supposed to be.

"*You* can hear and probably see the difference if a motor is out of kilter.

"What is the difference, in the long run, between what you do and what I do? I am merely better at one. You are better at the other. Together, we make one whale of a team!" His eyes glistened with pride in our newly formed partnership.

"Roy, if you took this much time to try and teach me about car motors, I could probably tear one apart on my own — after years and years of practice. But, please stand by, just in case I cannot get the dern thing back together again!

"You are on my turf here, Mr. Caddell. I would be on your turf there, and I'd probably flunk! Take heart, you are doing great." He beamed.

Roy's early fascination with "big wordts" was a two-edged sword that did no harm to anyone. Quite the opposite.

His initial mistaken belief that, "them's the ones I don't know how'ta spell," rapidly became illusion when, months and months down the road, he came to the slow realization that, "it's them little wordts that is the hard-est f'r me. And they shouldt be the easist! That makes me madt at myself."

So, in fact, he ascertained his needs. I did not point them out to him. This was frequently the case with this man. And, isn't that really the best way?

"I just love them big ole words — it shows me I fi-nally got some ed-ucashun. People like me don't wanna learnt the little words we might al-readty know. We wanna go where we ain't been, 'ta mix w'th the high-class folks that are ed-ucat'dt."

As we slowly and meticulously tore the remaining words apart, then labored to put them together again — much like Humpty Dumpty, I could not help but think how impossible this must all seem to a simple man from the country.

Amazing what three short hours could both sow and reap. For this one man, food for a lifetime.

Improbable as it might now seem, the Words Within Words exercise was the key that ultimately unlocked Roy Caddell. Every single time I placed my hands over parts of words to reveal another tiny word tucked inside, he was encouraged. Yes, I know many words are not pronounced as the internal words might dictate. But when you are at the bottom and climbing up, *any* foothold is welcome. Anything is better than nothing.

When I initially showed him "AT" inside CONVERSATION and asked him to "please read this to me," his retort was "At?" Total shock and utter disbelief. When I then moved my hand further back to reveal "SAT," he was taken aback. Surely, it could not be this easy.

But, over much time and literally thousands of instances where I covered various parts of almost every word we encountered that first year, he came to believe that *"maybe, just maybe I can do this."* He came to realize that parts of this convoluted Reading Business can be friendly.

Here were simple mechanics. Mechanics and tools Roy Caddell understood. He loved tearing an engine apart, finding out what was wrong, fixing it — then putting it back together again, to run like a spinning top.

We used the same exact process with words, another lateral and logical progression. This was what we did together every day, as a team. We made the English language run like a well-oiled machine.

Auto mechanics. Word mechanics. We could've hung out our shingles.

At this juncture, toward the end of June, this man's adventure into reading and writing encompassed not yet two short months, eighteen class sessions. He was right. He still wrestled with tiny words, which made him angry at himself. It also flustered and embarrassed him, which grieved me. For now, I said nothing.

Here I sat, having expended my entire lifetime learning. Roy Caddell had but one *fifty-hour work week* to his credit. Shocking. The chasm between us was unfathomable.

He could not read because he could not recognize simple words like NO, NOT, WITH, THAT, WHO, WHAT, WHEN, WHERE, HOW, THEN, THEY, ONE, ON, A, AN, AND, FOR, FROM, GO, ME, YOU, HIM, HER, WE, US, OUR, ARE, OWN, RUN, RAN, NOW.

Such enumeration is endless. Every tutor has such a catalogue of similar words from their students. Our lists go on and on, as do their struggles.

Roy and I addressed spelling every single day, one way or another. I stressed sounds. He strained to pronounce them. I stressed base pronunciation. He labored to make his mouth work correctly.

He was absolutely right. The little words were killers for him, which dumbfounded me. These about "did him in." Even today, four years hence, he misses some occasionally.

These alone were a lesson in humility and compassion I shall ever remember, with anguish and admiration for this one man.

He was the tenacious one in our classroom.

GOOD NEWS AND
BAD NEWS

"Still 'n all, Trude, ya'd think
them high-ly ed-ucat'dt people
couldt get it right. I'm serious
now. This here ain't funny. That
guy that made't all them up? He
had'ta have somethin' bad wrong
w'th him. No one wouldt do this
'xcept outta mean-ness."

Roy Caddell did not like words that sound alike. The "Big Boys" call them "homonyms." The Big Boys are strictly the Educated People.

From Roy's perspective, which certainly has merit, homonyms were put into the English language only to confuse. To him, they made "absolute-ly no sense't, I do not understandt it. This here is dumb! Why, them people that made't up all them words? There must a been somethin' bad wrong w'th them that day. Why couldtn't they have jist used't one a them words f'r ever'thing? 'Spec-ially since't they all soundt 'x-actly the same! It's dumb, I tell you. Stupid dumb!" I smiled as I sat there thinking. He caught only the smile.

"I'm serious, Trude. Why wouldt people go in 'n mess up a per-fectly good i-dear, when one a them wordts woulda work'dt f'r all a them words? I'd shore like'ta know where all this comes from — and I'd shore like'ta git my hands on them fellers that made't this up! Boy, what I wouldtn't like'ta do 'ta them!"

"TRUDE, IT DON'T TAKE NO BRAINS 'TA KNOWT I TALK DIFF'RENT FROM YOU. NOW YOU CAN CALL IT WHAT YOU WANT, BUT I'M ALWAYS GONNA SOUNDT COUNTRY. 'TA ME, THAT'S A POLITE WAY A SAYIN' HILLBILLY."

This was not the first time Roy Caddell had queried, "Who start'dt this all anyways?" Inquisition had set in soon after lessons began. As time passed, defiance rose. Now he was ready to wage war against the unseen foe who was making his life miserable.

I did not have answers to my friend's excellent, but potent questions. It had been a very long time since I had considered the origins of language. Perhaps, I needed to look into these for him.

Because I am neither a student of languages nor a scholar, Roy and I together sought help from our good friend Wally Waits at the library. He gave insight and pointed us to much literature available on the subject. I chose not to confuse the issue terribly and settled on the barest of data.

Roy and I learned of that time in European history known as the Middle Ages — from the fall of the Roman Empire, approximately A.D. 476 — to the demise of the Eastern Empire of Rome, with the Fall of Constantinople in 1453.

We learned of the Romance languages used during this time frame, and how narrative ballads were sung regaling romantic adventures in love and war. These sometimes fictitious songs became the oral traditions of their countries, and were verbally passed from village to village, circulated among the people. Embellishment was the order of the day and rapidly became fact.

Roy learned that few people in this era could read or write, be they nobility or common folk. Romance languages became diluted and impacted with the language of the common man, a generally illiterate population. Commonplace vernacular later became accepted speech, the norm. What was spoken became what was written — hence, much of the world's slang. Like it or not, such words were here to stay.

All this loose interpretation meant only one thing to Roy Caddell. He still "sound'dt hillbilly." Common.

"Roy, whatever you want to call it, language is influenced by the people who speak it, where they live and their life circumstances.

"What I think is being explained here, is that in one part of the world, a word may mean one thing, but elsewhere — in another village or even in another country — a word with the exact same pronunciation might mean something altogether different.

"Written language did not happen all at once, Mr. Caddell. It evolved slowly. Somewhere along the way, words began to have multiple meanings to different peoples around the world.

"We both know that countless words in dictionaries have more than one meaning, you have gleaned that repeatedly for yourself. Are we supposed to leave one meaning out, yet include another?

"We are right back to Square One, Roy. We only have twenty-six letters in our alphabet to make over a million words. Long ago, you thought there would be more. The same applies here with the words that form our language.

"Who is to say what goes and what stays? Who is to say why one word is spelled one way, while another one — that sounds exactly the same — is spelled quite differently and has a different meaning?

"You tell me, which do we include and which do we leave out? You be the judge on this one. . . ." He sat shaking his head in utter contempt.

By now, he knew there was no one answer. There rarely is. Fortunately, he comprehended these general facts. *He* was the one wanting to know why our language was in the shape it is — a mess.

"Still 'n all, Trude, you'd think them high-ly ed-ucat'dt people couldt get it right." The man had a good point.

However, the bottom line remained: I had to find some way to make this palatable for my friend. Unless he accepted the fact that homonyms were here to stay, he would be in real trouble. He would never learn to read and write. *That* would kill my very soul.

CAPITOL and CAPITAL were the first two comrades to breeze into our lives. They were big words, hard words. They did not stay long, I kept right on going. None of this was in my teacher's text.

RIGHT and WRITE were another matter. They hit us head on, early on. They could not be ignored. These two words were here to stay and, instinctively, he knew it.

On this lesson day, late in our first workbook — when THINK and THANK had been used as example words for beginning sounds in Lesson Ten — I chose to tackle the concept of homonyms. We would run the word gamut thus far, and either he would leave or he would stay.

"Mr. Caddell, do you know how to spell what we are working on? The word WRITE?"

"Shore. It's just like your right handt. Ain't it?"

"Well. As a matter of fact, it is not. The WRITE we are talking about, and what you are doing with your RIGHT hand, is spelled W-R-I-T-E. I knew you would be thrilled to hear this news."

"Now, Trude. If this here is a joke, it ain't funny."

"It is not a joke, but it *is* comical. As my husband says, it's called 'the Good News and the Bad News.'" He immediately raised his eyebrows and looked dubious.

"What's the good news? I ain't heard any so far."

"The good news is: You will learn to love this word, if for no other reason than what you W-R-I-T-E will give you away. Someday, somewhere, someone will catch a glimpse of what you have written, Sir. You know they will. And *that* can expose your secret." *That* got his attention.

"Trude. I'm not ever gonna *love* this here word. No ways. I'm tellin' you now, them words ain't friendt-ly."

"Fair enough. You will at least learn to like this word."

"That's more like it. Now. What's your bad news?" he sullenly stabbed in my direction.

"There are three of these little devils, RIGHT, WRITE and RITE. More bad news: All three are pronounced exactly the same way. Still more bad news: All three have different meanings. Even more bad news: All three are spelled differently!" I was grinning. He was not. He looked thunderstruck.

"They shoulda shot the guy that made't all them up." I dissolved into gales of laughter. He did not. With that, we began.

RIGHT he knew — even how to spell — which was no small miracle. But WRITE was not even in the same ballpark in which he played. He could not have caught that word had it been driven into his glove. He would not have thrown home, he would have stood gawking at this unwanted foreign obstruction.

"There is no easy way around these, Roy. You simply must memorize them. R-I-G-H-T you already know. So forget that for now.

"WRITE is not the enemy. It wants to be your friend. Once you learn W-R-I-T-E, you will know R-I-T-E. All you do is leave off the first letter. That W in W-R-I-T-E is silent, you do not hear it. Just like the silent Es and Ys we have dealt with in other words.

"I think that's what gives you trouble here, the letter that you cannot hear. No one hears these silent devils, remember that. But, we all see the letter W on the word. We cannot leave it off." With that, I crossed out W on our worksheet and, sure enough, there was R-I-T-E before him.

"Well, now. That ain't so hard. Sure-ly I can r'member that," and he studied both words for a moment.

"RIGHT, WRITE and RITE," I repeated once again. "The last RITE meaning 'rite of passage, coming of age.' As in Judaism, when a young boy or girl reaches the age for Bar Mitzvah, for boys — or Bat Mitzvah, as it is called for girls."

"Yeah. I heard a that, I think."

"I thought you would have, that is why I am including this. Because R-I-T-E is a word you will rarely use, if ever, like BOVINE. But, it is a word you need to be familiar with, how to spell and recognize, either in print or if someone else is speaking of it in conversation." He sat quietly, pondering. Finally, he spoke.

"What you're a tellin' me here is that WRITE is right, ain't that it?"

"That is exactly what I am telling you, Sir! But how did you so quickly zero in on that?" My mouth was agape.

"Well. When you 'x-plain it all this way, it makes sense't. Trude, I have learnt one thing in my goin' along. You don't learn much if you always ignore somethin'.

"I done triedt that in my other life. It don't help none. Things don't just up 'n go away. In my past life, befor' this here, I'da rather chang'dt the subject when I din't know somethin'.

"But it ain't any good if you're al-ways coverin' up. I done that all my life with humor, 'n look where that's got me. So's, I might as well git at it. I think I know what you're tellin' me. I seen them two words plenty a times, I just never knowt what they meant.

"Still 'n all, Trude," he continued as he turned to face me with an impish grin and twinkling eyes, "You aren't never gonna go down to that corner out there 'n WRITE me a note with your RIGHT hand while you're turnin' RIGHT. You ain't never gonna do that, no-body is.

"Hmmph. One of them words woulda been plenty f'r me. I couldt say ever'thing I want'dt to w'th just one word. I'm tellin' you, they mess'dt up now."

Perhaps *they* did. I could not argue against him. Again, we had stemmed the tide on a potentially volatile issue. I breathed a sigh of relief.

Slowly, he made progress on the three little devils. It was no small feat. It took, literally, months. Even today, if he is in a hurry, or tired or upset, he will revert to old comfortable habits. RIGHT becomes RITE; WRITE becomes RIGHT.

Never would I have dreamed of such difficulty. No wonder I never knew where our lessons would take us. This modest man charted the course. I merely tried to navigate treacherous waters, and I am a dern good swimmer. There were times I nearly drowned.

Roy Caddell did not like RIGHT, WRITE and RITE. But, he did not hate them either. SALE and SAIL he hated, with a passion and a vengeance. On the positive side, RIGHT and WRITE had merit to them. He could see their necessity. WRITE was what he had come to learn.

SALE and SAIL had only negatives on their side, with a capital N — for "Nasty." His word, not mine.

Today I decided to get all of the bad news out of the way at once. I told him there were two more of these little critters that sounded almost identical to SALE and SAIL: CELL and SELL. I wrote both on his paper, beside the others. There was "no joy in Mudville." Roy took one look and turned to me with fire in his eyes. He spat anger with his words.

"What was wrong w'th that guy anyways? Was he drunk that day?" With that, I was once again on the floor, laughing. He never cracked a smile.

"I'm serious now. This here ain't funny. That guy that made't all them up? He had'ta have somethin' bad wrong w'th him. *No one wouldt do this 'xcept outta mean-ness.* They all sound 'x-actly the same 'ta me." Finally, I found my voice.

"Roy, you know I do not know the answers to your questions. I wish I did. I would like to make this easier for you. At least I did not tell you about these four musketeers the day we had the story about Mrs. Bell selling her eggs. I thought about it, and passed."

"Well. I shore do thank you f'r that!"

"I told you there was good news." He grinned sheepishly and shook his head.

"This here is gonna be a confusin' lesson. I can see that al-readty."

For Roy Caddell, it was. He could not believe supposedly educated and highly intelligent people would have made such a grievous error. To him, there was "simp-ly no 'x-cuse't f'r it. Not when one wordt woulda done f'r all a them. I do not understandt it. I thought them TWOs were gonna be the only-est ones. I can tell now I was wrong."

He shook his head, angry. Angry at the horrid, malevolent prank being played on him. Angry at the audacity of learned men to intentionally inflict such trickery and pain on others — because homonyms pained Roy Caddell. Not that they existed, but that people *really* talked that way, and he had never even known it. Finally, he softly spoke.

"Are you a tellin me that them other people talk so's you can tell somethin' strange 'bout them four words when you say 'em?"

"Yes, Sir. That is exactly what I am telling you."

"I was afear'dta that. . . ."

Now do you understand why I have been stressing sounds and pronunciations so diligently, over and over? Why your own enunciation is so vitally important? For you! To train your hearing and your ear. I don't give a hang what anyone else speaks or hears. I bloody well do care what you speak and hear!

"There are tiny variables in countless English words, Roy. They appear unfriendly. Perhaps they are. But what you hear is what you will repeat. I desperately want you to understand others, and others to understand you. This is a two-way street. Don't ever forget that."

"Then, we might as well git at it." So we did.

Slowly, homonyms moved from this man's "Do Not Like" column into the neutral abyss signifying neither desolation nor hope. It just is.

From time to time, on subsequent homework papers, I would find he had written these "nasty,

"THEM HOMONYMS ARE LIKE KISSIN' Y'UR SISTER. DON'T WANNA DO IT TOO OFTEN. SOMEBODY'S LUCKY IF THEY ONLY GOT ONE SISTER . . . OUGHTTA BE THAT WAY W'TH THEM WORDS THAT SOUNDT ALIKE. ONE WOULDT DO."

dumb, bad, dirty, rotten" words amongst reams of others, without additional comment.

I would smile to myself and be thankful we had tackled these when we did. They would serve this man well the rest of his days, and ultimately become friends. But, once again, he *WROTE* it best. . . .

"I'm gonna like these little devils in about ten years."

It was Square One all over again. We could no longer avoid THINK and THANK. Roy pronounced them exactly the same and, in his mind, they were. These two words he did not hate, or even intensely dislike. He simply felt they were wasted letters.

Now, I know these words are not homonyms. But to Roy, they were "kissin' cousins that ya knowt were in the same family, but ya shore e'nuff don't knowt all their names." His words, not mine.

"Why wouldt anyone in their right mindt go 'n mess somethin' up that don't need botherin' w'th?" He crossed his arms in disgust as I wrote THINK and THANK on his paper and turned to look at him.

Like RIGHT and WRITE, he knew he *needed* these words. So, we went to work again — and again, he got it. Slowly.

Even with the obvious tiny word INK shouting out to him from THINK, it was difficult. Although it was a word he often used, THINK was not in his vocabulary. For him, it did not exist. THANK was his "one-size-fits-all."

Continually I heard: "I'll *thank* 'bout it. *Thank* it'll make me any difference? *Thank* I'll go run me an er-randt. I *thank* I'm a learnin' somethin' after all. *Thank* you."

Although I never corrected his diction on the two words, I repeated his sentences back to him correctly whenever possible. It had never taken, until today. Finally, it clicked.

"What you're tellin' me here, Trude, is that you can say 'em any way you want to — but, you cain't write 'em but one way? Ain't that it?"

"Yes, Sir. That is exactly what I am telling you. I do not care how you say these two words, as long as you can make yourself understood. But, I do care how you write these two words. Your everyday pronunciation is not my focus now. But, the way you spell these words and, that you *hear* a difference between the two, most certainly is."

"I can shore understandt that," he acknowledged."Befor' today, I'd al-ways go to the only one I knowt. And forget about them others. That's the only-est way I couldt make it, Trude.

"I had'ta listen in on how them other people talk, and then try 'n get what words I couldt from their con-versashuns. But I couldt not get all their wordts at onc'dt. I tri'dt, but I couldt not never do it.

"I know now there's a difference in them two wordts. That's the im-port'nt-estst part right there. I feel like I'm on my ways." He was satisfied. I was satiated.

Perception. This man had it in spades. He knew himself as few people do. He knew his own deficits. Humankind could learn much from this man.

"I DON'T KNOWT IF THEM ED-UCAT'DT PEOPLE WERE TRYIN' 'TA HURT ME 'R NOT. BUT IN MY MINDT, THEY WERE — AND I DIN'T LIKE THAT. THE ONLY REASON I DO ALL THIS IS BECAUSE I DO NOT WANT 'TA STAY THE WAY I WAS."

Hatbands and Numbers

*"I know you are coming back.
But, for many people who come
to learn to read, they might
never make it through this first
workbook, for circmstances
beyond their control. From my
perspective, you need these extra
benefits I throw out constantly.
Now. Not in six weeks or six
months."*

"We survive any way we can. We git mad a lot. It's a terrible feelin'. Survival at home is to put ever'thing ov'r on your spouse, like payin' the bills 'n readin' the mail. You don't never feel like you're doin' your part."

Coupled with Roy not knowing his own address, the fact that he did not know his numbers was a shock, because I knew he handled money. Roy Caddell was very careful with his money. The fact that he could not *read* numbers did not surprise me. But not knowing numerical numerals past one hundred? That floored me. My naiveté at times definitely handicapped us.

In all objectivity, numbers in written form make absolutely no sense. There is no discernable logic to them, no consistency, no rhythm, no pattern, no basis — nothing on which to hang your hat.

How does a tutor explain to a student that two becomes twelve, then twenty? And twenty becomes two hundred, and two hundred becomes two thousand? Or three becomes thirteen, then thirty? Or try four and forty. Or five and fifteen, or fifteen becomes fifty.

These are difficult concepts to people like my friend. They are simply illogical to us. Such numerically written increments threw this man into reverse.

He thought I was jesting, that surely this was another ruse and definitely "not funny." I only could smile, as there was no logical explanation. It just *was*.

"What were them guys thinkin' of, Trude?" he thundered. "This makes ab-solutely no sense ne'ther. It makes me madt all over again."

"You know I do not have answers for your potent questions. But, if ever I see *them guys*, I shall ask what they were thinking when they made all this up. Obviously, they were having a very bad day!" He grinned at my sarcasm.

Since numbers were the thrust of Lessons Eleven and Twelve, and very wisely included in our texts, we began again.

The comma that separates groupings of three numerical digits meant nothing to this man. Not one thing. He merely thought it was another displaced punctuation mark, permanently lost.

"You mean, that that there pause is tellin' me somethin'? That after that, I'm into them thousandts? And ten thousandts? Why didn't they just say so? Hrmph." And he folded his arms in total exasperation.

"They are saying that, Roy. That is exactly what *them guys* are trying to tell you, in perhaps the only way they knew how. Each of those little commas *does* imply importance. Unless, of course, you are dying to give your money away." *That* got his attention!

We went over and over numbers and their complicated, "unfriendt-ly" spellings. Day after day, Roy laboriously wrote out various numerals on lengthy homework papers. Day after day, I would point randomly to what he had written and ask him what the number was.

Some he could readily tell me. Others, he could not. For weeks and weeks, numbers like forty, nineteen, thirty-three, fifty-five and twelve — perhaps the hardest of all — tripped him up.

We kept at it until slowly, slowly he could recognize the numbers up to and including, one thousand. After that, his feelings were simple: "I ain't never gonna need'ta write nuthin' that big, Trude. So's if I sees one comin' at me like that, I'm gonna run real quick-like and get me some help. I'll needt it." His eyes twinkled as he turned to grin at me.

Finally, he was pleased with his newly acquired knowledge, however hard earned. But, he saw a pothole in our roadway.

"Trude," he said, growing solemn, "I'm never gonna give up on these numbers. So's you'll just haf'ta bear w'th me if I'm not doin' so goodt some days. I gots me the desire to go faster, so I can see where I been. I al-ways like things best after their finish'dt. But sum'a this still makes me nervous. This here is one. I think what I'm real-ly tryin'ta say is, I'm shore sorry *f'r you* we cain't go faster."

"Roy, we have a big problem here. I do not know how you can go any faster, because I do not know how I can teach you any faster. You keep me at a dead run as it is, trying to stay ahead of you.

"Now. If you have a suggestion on this matter, Friend, I need to hear it. I am the one needing help. You, Sir, keep working on your numbers and we will both be fine." I hurled my grin toward his somber face. He caught it and warmly smiled back.

Numbers never appeared on Roy Caddell's wrist. But, I would not have been surprised if he had tucked away a tiny list inside his worn billfold or hat band, just in case.

After all, you "never knowt when a fella's gonna needt a little nudge."

With numbers like twenty-one, twenty-two, twenty-three, twenty-four, twenty-five, twenty-six, twenty-seven, twenty-eight and twenty-nine, and upwards in such increments, we introduced the hyphen and the hyphenated word. Roy had heard of neither, though he obviously had seen hyphens.

"All this means, Sir, is that these numbers go together. They are connected by that tiny dash you see between the two numbers. Connected every time, like a bridge joins two parcels of land. Here, though, that bridge is called a 'hyphen.' One short dash, that's all you have to remember.

"When two words make up a single number and they're joined by one of these hyphen marks, like twenty-seven, it's called a 'hyphenated word.' You cannot have the second word in such numbers without that hyphen. It would have no meaning, just as no address is complete without that zip code."

"Yeah. I think I fine-ly got that one down, I still been workin' on it though." Fortunately, he grinned.

"Well. Now you can work on these. Two numbers, one dash. Two parts, one whole. You cannot have one without the other."

"What y'ur a tellin' me here, Trude, is that I gotta be watchin' out f'r that little stuff. Pay at-tenshun."

"That is exactly what I am telling you, Mr. Caddell. The little *stuff*, as you call it, is terribly important. I am not sitting here telling you all this for my health — which is fine, thank you."

Because hyphenated words were a focus of Lesson Twelve, I elected to include compound words in our lesson for today. We had looked at the word *Homework* for two long months. I felt my friend deserved to know what that word was. After all, he was certainly knowledgeable about work — he had spent his whole life doing it.

"Compound words in our English language mean two separate words joined together to form one word, one meaning — no hyphen. These words are *not* hyphenated words, Roy." Turning his yellow legal tablet towards me, I began writing.

"Examples of compound words are: SCHOOLHOUSE, WITHIN, WITHOUT, BASEBALL, FOOTBALL, CLASSROOM, HOMEROOM, HOUSEWORK, WORKBOOK, CHECKBOOK, WATERMELON, BARNYARD, SCHOOLYARD and FRIENDSHIP. We use such words constantly. Why they exist in our language, I do not know. But they can be most helpful."

"Hmmm. I see what you mean. Two f'r one. I seen 'em al-right, but I never knowt why they was the way they are. I'll haf'ta start lookin' f'r them."

Which, of course, he did. He still uses the term, "two f'r one," to this day, though he knows they are correctly called compound words. I do not correct him. We both know what he means.

I further explained the word *compound* does not apply only to words. Compounds can run the whole gamut of our language and society.

"Compounds can apply to money and interest, math. Compounds can apply to science, chemistry, animals. Your cows all have *compound* stomachs, as in more than one. In the case of cows, they have two.

"Compound can also apply to problems, difficulties with people or things. Quarrels can be compounded, or enlarged — just as can rumors, or unkind words." He quickly got my meaning.

"I heard you there. I knowt that about a cow, but I never knowt what it was called."

"Well. Now you do. Like I tell my friends, if they have a decorating question on design or color, or how something will look after the fact, use me before. I am telling you the same thing, Mr. Caddell. Use me all you can. Ask me anything, that is why I am here." He grinned widely as I continued.

"The interesting thing about compound words is that each word combined is equally important. You cannot leave one out, the entire meaning would be forever altered. Compound words need the two parts.

"Just as with us, neither is more important than the other. You would not be sitting here without a teacher — in this case, me. I would not be sitting here without a student — in this case, you. Compound *need*. So, too, with words and letters, Mr. Caddell. Back to Square One."

"Yeah. But, I ain't never had nobody 'ta tell me all this befor'. So, I just skipp'dt over it 'n went on. You shore don't learn much doin' that too often."

"No, Sir. You do not. That is why I try to leave nothing out. You need it. If not now, then later. And, in all honesty, you needed it years and years ago." He nodded his head affirmatively.

"To me, Roy, it seems our first workbook has omitted a great deal of important material. I do not like that, for you or for others. This might be your only exposure to much of this information.

"Like President Harry S. Truman said, 'The buck stops here.' The same applies to me. I am, perhaps, your last resort. I am responsible both for what you learn — and what you do not learn.

"Another major factor to be considered here is that I know you are coming back. But, for many people who come to learn to read, they might never make it through this first workbook, for circumstances beyond their control.

"From my perspective, you *need* these extra benefits I throw out constantly. *Now*. Not in six weeks or six months. I could drop dead tomorrow, and where would that leave you?" He pondered a moment before answering, but only that. He had considered this very thing. Intelligent.

"I knowt what you mean. It's like I was tellin' Hazel the other mornin'. If somethin' was to happen, I'm real gladt I came. I like the learnin' part, I shore do. 'Cause I needt it, like you say. But, I like the talkin' part, too.

"I like comin' down here 'n tellin' you all this stuff. I ain't never talk'dt this much in my whole life. I guess 'cause I ain't never had't a best friend befor'. It shore 'nuff is a miracle." He turned to smile wistfully, almost embarrassed by his own words.

"You know, Trude. You been tellin' me over 'n over how all this wants to be friend-ly, it wants me to like it. How you sorta look on words 'n doin' all this as your friends. Well, I been thinkin' 'bout that. And I'm tryin'ta look at it the same way — as friends. I shore never thought I'd get there, but I think maybe it's a helpin' me." He was lost in thought.

Amazing. One never knows when they plant a seed, what will grow, or where. I never once thought my myriad ramblings would be any more than passing comments to Roy Caddell. Wrong.

Here was a man who had spent his life searching and probing, yet getting nowhere. Here was a man who had unanswered questions, and unexposed fears. Here was a man who was a complex puzzle whose pieces did not yet fit.

He had made more than one friend in this bargain, words and me. It was almost more than he could comprehend.

GIBBERISH AND THE REAL McCoy

They say that laughter is good for the soul, that its
medicine both helps and heals. Not a day went by that
I did not laugh uproariously from some innocent,
innocuous uttering of Roy Caddell's.

Lesson Thirteen's coverage of the possessive case was a cakewalk for Roy Caddell. Probably because we had covered this when I first gave him a dictionary six weeks earlier. Whatever he thought of that dictionary then, mattered not at all as we approached this last lesson in the first workbook. What he *had* remembered that long ago day was that, henceforth, the book was his possession.

"OK, Friend. This you are going to like. This is simple." And I wrote on his paper, on succeeding lines, these three things:

Sam has a pup.
This is Sam's pup.
This is his pup.

The first two were in my teacher's text, the last I added. To me, it was like a dangling participle: Sooner or later it must be corrected, or in this case, included. He watched me finish writing.

"These three sentences mean exactly the same thing, Roy. They only differ in how you say that this person Sam owns that pup. All three sentences show possession or ownership.

"The sole distinguishing characteristic among the three is the tiny little mark in the second sentence called an 'apostrophe.' That apostrophe is always elevated like this," I stressed, pointing to the 's. The mark looks rather like a comma suspended in air.

"Remember the day I wrote ROY'S HAT? The same applies here with SAM'S PUP. You own your hat, Sam owns his dog. I could just as easily have written:

Roy has a hat.
This is Roy's hat.
This is his hat.

"All I am telling you here, Sir, is that there is more than one way to skin a cat."

"You mean that's all there is? Them three things with that little high-up comma mark there? I see what you're doin' here, Trude. Shore-ly, I can r'member that." He remembered.

"Now, please pronounce the word *apostrophe* for me, Roy." It was hard. He dropped his lower jaw as he strained to enunciate, "A-*postropheee*" several times. His pronunciation was good enough for me, it wasn't likely to be a word he would use too often.

"Generally, Roy, apostrophe marks are followed by the letter S; as in 'S. Sometimes, however, with plural nouns, the apostrophe follows the letter S. As in 'The Caddells' house.' You and Hazel own that house jointly, so the apostrophe mark follows the plural ending. The same would apply to 'The Normans' house.'" He nodded affirmatively as I finished writing the phrases.

There was seldom a time after this when he did not recall what "that little high-up mark" meant. I would take it any way he remembered it.

Other facets of the possessive case spelled trouble for Roy Caddell: They were irritating to him and caused him much agitation. Take the basic sentence, "This library conference room is OUR room to use."

OUR sounds very similar to ARE in everyday conversation. Roy pronounced both the same. ARE he could say, but he could seldom spell correctly. Usually, he spelled it A-R. So, for us to advance from ARE to OUR was no small task.

If an adult does not know one of the basic cornerstones of writing and conversation — the word ARE, how do they suddenly grasp OUR, when they are fifty years behind? It was hard for Roy. I did not make a federal case out of either.

In actuality, we worked on ARE for months on end. Occasionally, he still has trouble with the word. Looking back, ARE is a word Roy and I should have focused on from the onset of lessons. It was not included in my teacher's text; and, at that point in time, I assumed Roy knew this word. Once again, I was wrong.

THEIR and THERE presented similar problems for this man — only in triplicate. He hated these words! Take the sentence, "That is THEIR house over THERE." From his standpoint, we were back to homonyms. Treacherous. There were times he must have felt he was swimming with sharks.

"Now, Trude. Them last two ain't friendt-ly. I'm gonna put 'em in my *Do Not Like* column. That is dumb! One wordt woulda work'dt f'r both of them, why din't they just try that first?"

I let him vent, I had no answers. Four years later, we are still working on these two words.

Or, throw in THEY ARE in its contractual form, THEY'RE. Coupled with THEIR and THERE, THEY'RE nearly did him in. How could he grasp this when he struggled daily to clarify ARE in his own mind? It was another "catch 22" every tutor and student face.

Make no mistake about it, some of this Roy Caddell did not like, but he knew that he must have a grasp of these facets of language. They were his lifeline, and the link to the outside world from which he had been excluded for sixty long years.

So, while he was vocal about "That Which He Did Not Like," he was equally verbose about "That Which He Did Like."

> He liked knowing the parts of speech, and how to pronounce each.
> He liked knowing every sentence begins with a capital letter and ends "w'th one a them little marks."
> He liked knowing words from his world, like BOVINE.
> He liked knowing big words, from any world.
> He liked knowing small words that had previously eluded him.

"I JUST USED ONE A THEM. I DIN'T KNOW THEY WAS SPELL'DT DIFF'RENT. I DIN'T KNOW 'N I DIN'T CARE. WHY WORRY 'BOUT THERE WHEN THERE WAS ALL THESE OTHER THINGS I DIN'T KNOW?"

He liked knowing numbers, the ones that "made't sens'dt."
He liked knowing correct pronunciations, especially for big words.
He liked knowing punctuation.
He liked knowing he can write in cursive, and not embarrass himself.
He liked knowing he can write better than his teacher can write. Not
*   a fair contest from my perspective!*
He liked knowing the mechanics of spelling.
He liked knowing consonant blends.
He liked knowing hard words he deemed important — like
*   FLUTTERED, TELEPHONE, PHYSICIAN, WHISTLE.*
He liked knowing he could read road signs.
He liked knowing he can challenge his wife on quiz shows.
He liked knowing he can pick up a daily newspaper. Finally.
He liked knowing he can better understand conversations.
He liked knowing he can participate in conversations.
He liked knowing he can better understand the spoken word.
He liked knowing he was now widening his mental parameters.
He liked knowing he could begin to stop making war with our
*   convoluted English language.*
He liked knowing he could make friends.
He loved knowing the alphabet!
He loved knowing he could read something!
He liked knowing he can like at least one lawyer.

But above all, my biased summation is that Roy Caddell liked knowing an "educated person" who would talk with him, not at him or through him as if he were not there. A person who would look him in the eye and explain things, with patience and kindness, without condescension. One who would not treat him as less than, but, rather, as more than. As an equal, a friend. Little did he know that it was my greatest privilege.

Next we tackled a concept I call Word Conjugation. There are perhaps thousands of words in our English language which Roy Caddell could master. But first, he had to *see* that he could. He had to see that parts of this Education Business were neither difficult nor tedious, but fun. What I envisioned was much like a science fair, a hands-on approach — touch, see, feel, learn and, most of all, enjoy. For us, it was another logical progression.

Throughout my teacher's text we had been given simple words to use in questions concerning enunciation, consonant blends, speech and sounds. We applied such words as directed for weeks on end.

Each of these chosen words for our new game was marvelous for two reasons: *One.* They were short. *Two.* They all had vowels as their middle letter. Imperative!

These were my guinea pigs, taken directly from my teacher's text: BOY, CUP, MAN, LEG, PAN, FUN, BIG, BED, CAR, BOX, CAB, GAS, HAT, RED, JOB, BIG, JUG, LIP, HAM, MET, NUT, NAP, FAT, PUP, TOP, SOB, RUN, WAS, SIX, FOX, HOT, PET, SIT, BUS, HAS, HIS, COP, MOP, NOT, GET, HAD, JAR, JAM, KEY, PEG, BAG, DOG, ROB, HOP and ZIP.

As we neared the end of our first book, it struck me that untold numbers of these tiny words held magic. They were not as they appeared. They were hidden gold, treasures waiting to be unearthed, which was exactly what I intended to do.

We were into the study of short vowels and their respective sounds. This day, we were working with only A, E, I, O and U. I had Roy make five columns across his page, each headed by one of these five vowels.

We would take one simple word, such as BAG, and magically transform it by switching vowels. We would see what new words we could make if only one tiny letter were changed — the middle letter, the vowel! Roy had to try and use each vowel shown to make an actual word.

Thus, our papers looked like this:

<u>A</u>	<u>E</u>	<u>I</u>	<u>O</u>	<u>U</u>
BAG	BEG	BIG	BOG	BUG
HAT	HET	HIT	HOT	HUT
HAM	HEM	HIM	HOM	HUM
HAP	HEP	HIP	HOP	HUP
MAP	MEP	MIP	MOP	MUP
NAT	NET	NIT	NOT	NUT
RAN	REN	RIN	RON	RUN
CAP	CEP	CIP	COP	CUP
PAN	PEN	PIN	PON	PUN

As those of you who read quickly can ascertain, not all of these "words" are words — the whole point of the exercise. Some are, some are not.

Roy Caddell did not know which were and which were not. He had seldom seen these words written. Most were but mere letters to him. At this point in our lessons, he did not trust himself enough to differentiate between The Real McCoy and gibberish.

The bottom line question became: "Are they, or aren't they?" *I* would not tell. Which left him two alternatives: His dictionary, or his best guess.

We read through the entire listing together. I pointed to appropriate columns as I pronounced each word. Then, I turned to Roy with a blank face. He would have to discern which were words and which were not.

To get him started, I helped him with the first line across, telling him they were actual words and each was spelled correctly. These he did not have to look up in his dictionary.

But, *before this exercise, he had no idea how even these were spelled!* As he wrote each word on his tablet, he increased his written vocabulary and his writing skills, positives.

After the first line, I left the rest of the words to Roy and his dictionary.

"Boy. You ain't a gonna help me none w'th these, are you?"

"Not if I can help it, Mr. Caddell. These are simple words to look up. First, you have to try. If you find one of these words in your dictionary, the answer will be 'yes, it is a word.' If you do not find it, the answer will be 'no.' Yes or No. Your job."

Knowing any word he queried would have to be answered by himself or verified by his dictionary, it

"I'M AT LEAST AWARE OF THEM LETTERS NOW. I MIGHT NOT GIT 'EM ALL RIGHT, BUT I MIGHT NOT GIT 'EM WRONG. F'R ME, THAT'S PROGRESS."

did not take him long to stop looking to me for answers and start reaching for "that there book." He could find the ones he was unsure of himself, of that I was positive. It would simply take time.

So began our long-term association with Word Conjugation. So began Roy Caddell's labored affair with letters and words, and a mighty big book. *This is where this man began to soar with a dictionary!*

As he looked for a specific word, he came across others that interested him, on the same page or column where he was looking. Continually, he would stop and try to read what was written for another word definition. Many times my help was required.

Frequently, he made comments about words he stumbled across. Each "new" word quickly broadened his horizons. To me, this was why he had come to "school."

He had thought my Word Conjugation game would be a cut-and-dried assignment. I knew differently from the onset. The unfolding of this miracle will always be one of my fondest recollections — and one of Roy Caddell's most shocking revelations: He could do this work!

One day he looked at me and announced that he would not have to look up any of the five words: PAN, PEN, PIN, PON and PUN. I raised my eyebrows.

"Oh? How do you figure that, Sir?"

"Well. Them's all words, even I know that. We al-readty talk'dt 'bout that Punnin', so I know now that's a joke. And the rest a them I know."

"You are telling me that the other four are words, Mr. Caddell?"

"Yep."

"You are telling me that P-O-N is a word?"

"Yep."

"You are telling me that you have already looked that word up in your dictionary, and found it?"

"Don't need to."

"Oh, yes you do, Friend. P-O-N is not a word!" He whirled around to face me, his eyes as big as saucers. Total disbelief and shock were written across his face.

"What'a you mean? Ain't you never heard of no *Farm Pon?*" I absolutely dissolved on the floor in gales of laughter! Literally, I could not speak. Finally, he grinned, his face as red as a beet. He knew he had "been had."

"I can tell I better go in 'n look it up. I done got myself caught in that briar patch we was talkin' about earlier." Tears were streaming down my cheeks. He looked. I wept.

They say that laughter is good for the soul, its medicine both helps and heals. Not a day went by that I did not laugh uproariously from some innocent, innocuous uttering of Roy Caddell's.

He later confided, "I ain't never laugh'dt this much in my whole life, Trude. 'Special-ly not over somethin' this im-port'nt. I ain't never had this much fun w'th gittin' me an ed-ucashun."

The sheer unsophistication of a nonreader is a beautiful experience. They are completely without guile — except for what is needed for their absolute basic survival. Much as with an innocent child, only the cruelty of a small world crushes them.

Roy Caddell's inquisitive nature, his eagerness to seek out knowledge had placed us where we were. He was receptive to *anything* I chose to teach. His attitude was, "If I don't knowt them things, then I need'ta be learnin' 'em. That's why I come, Trude. 'Ta learn, and 'ta git me an ed-ucashun."

A wise Jewish rabbi, Menachem Mendel Schneerson, once said: "There are no dumb questions. Only selfish men who will not answer, or foolish men who could answer if only they would. I am not afraid to say that I don't know. . . . And if I do know, then I have no right not to answer." Roy liked that.

I liked best that he was now supplying some of his own answers.

Roy was excited about finishing this first workbook, but he was also "nervous as a cat." I was not sure why, so I asked him.

"'Cause I don't like them tests they give out. I done had e'nuff a them in my former life 'ta last me a lif'time." Of course.

"Roy, this is *not* a test where *you* get a grade. Before we move on to the next Laubach workbook, this is a series of questions to ascertain that I have done my job in teaching you. There is no pass or fail, except perhaps on me." He immediately brightened.

"Well. If you're shore. . . ."

"When I looked at the test several days ago, my guess was that you will scarcely miss a single question."

"Now *that* I'd like! Then I couldt go home 'n tell 'em how smart I am."

Before we arrived at the dreaded examination day, we had one more area I was determined to cover: Contractions — specifically, IT IS. This tiny contraction was listed number 300 in *Laubach's Tutor Workshop Handbook,* from the now familiar list of "300 Most Frequently Used Words." I was glad it was included. However, it was given with no explanation in the first workbook that I could find.

Roy Caddell liked apostrophes, "them little high-up marks." He thought they were fun. He also thought they showed class, learning and education. He wanted to be in all three categories. His feeling was, "I'm gonna git me sum'a them som'time." I did not ask which one.

One day I had read a fabulous article by a syndicated columnist which stated that IT IS is the most abused word in our language, as it is written in its contractual form, IT'S. I was amazed and appalled. Naturally, I cut the story out and brought it to Roy for our next lesson, whereupon we read the entire discourse together.

Sadly, when he took it home, it was lost — the only one of dozens to befall such a fate. I believe the author's name was James J. Kilpatrick, a noted columnist. I would like to give him full credit. It is my favorite writing on our bizarre language. His analogies were brilliant! My compliments.

The apostrophe in contractions, I explained to Roy, was a substitute for drawing together or shortening two separate words — nothing more, nothing less. That tiny mark "fills in" or takes the place of missing letters in countless English words.

Unless, of course, we are talking about possessives. Roy had "that a-postropheee" fairly clear in his own mind. I left well enough alone.

Now I wrote IT IS on his yellow paper and beside it, I wrote IT'S. He never blinked an eye.

"OK, Friend. This you will like. The apostrophe in this particular example is a substitute for one letter — an *I*, every single time, no exceptions." I wrote on his paper: "Apostrophe = I. Apostrophe = I. IT IS = IT'S. IT IS = IT'S. Always, always, always." I laid my pen down.

"That's it?"

"That's it."

"Well, I'll be. Now I see why sum'a this is try-in'ta be friendt-ly w'th me. Hmmm."

"You know, Trude. I was jist sittin' here thinkin', that learnin'ta readt is a whole lot like goin' blindt. It don't come on you all at onc'dt. It comes on you real slow-like, creepy-crawly." I felt my mouth drop open. I began writing as fast as I could, and still could not keep up, for laughing.

"You don't know ya cain't see nuthin' 'til you fine-ly get yourself one a them pairs a glasses. Then you know f'r sure. Yep. You're blindt al-right. Befor' them glasses, you think you can see. But you cain't. That's where I am right now. Needin' me some new glasses to see all y'ur tryin'ta teach me.

"When you first start learnin' them little ole dumb letters, you don't know f'r shore you don't know 'em. Just like you don't know f'r shore you cain't see. It all happens real slow-like.

"Then, pret-ty soon, you think maybe you *are* a goin' blindt. You go, 'Hey! I cain't see nuthin'!' But before that, you don't know f'r pos-tive you need glasses.

"Like, you think you know sum'a this here ed-ucashun. But you real-ly don't know nuthin'. What I'm a sayin' here is *I know now. I been blindt.*

"I don't like that part ne'ther, the dark spots. I don't wanna see a whole handful a this learnin' in bunches. I wanna see it all at onc'dt. I don't like them sleepy parts. I don't like knowin' nuthin', then find out I real-ly was just needin' me some new glasses. Boy. To think I been blindt all this time — 'n didn't even know it. That's bad."

My sides were splitting from laughter. Roy Caddell never had been the guest speaker, but he was warming up to the task. I let him go. He need-ed no encouragement.

"I CAN TELL THE TRUTH BY SAYIN' I CAIN'T SEE SOMETHIN' 'CAUSE I AIN'T PACKIN' MY GLASSES. I DON'T TAKE 'EM ANYWHERES BUT HERE. I GUESS THAT'S A PROTECTION OF MY FEAR A PEOPLE LEARNIN' ABOUT ME. I'M STILL SO ASHAM'DT. I DON'T WANNA BE BLINDT NO MORE, TRUDE. I DONE PUT IN MY TIME."

"One thing about it, Trude, I don't wanna be blindt. Nobody does. I'd like'ta have nuthin' but bright days aheadt. So, I'm gonna listen real good to what it is you're a tellin' me. I can tell now I'm gonna need it. I don't wanna al-ways be runnin' *from* them twenty-six letters. I wanna be runnin' *to* 'em."

"Oh, Roy. Those letters want you to like them. They truly do. They did not pick you out of a crowd to be mean to you. They did not suddenly say, *'Hey! Let's get the guy in the white hat.'*"

"I can tell that now, and I'm tryin'ta like them back. I think I knowt what you mean about them two IT'S. I seen 'em a bunch, wrote down both ways. I just never knowt what they meant.

"When I know how'ta read and write real goodt, all this'll make sense'ta me. It al-ready does, a little bit. But, what I can-not figur' out, is why I like it so much, why it's excitin'ta me still. I ain't never had nuthin' like this happen to me befor'. . . ."

Welcome to the club, Sir. Neither have I. You are an absolute first in anyone's book.

Throughout this soliloquy, my arm was falling off as I struggled to keep up with this man's words. My paper looked like hen scratches. I was laughing so much that I could barely hear what he was saying. My mind was awhirl. How simplistic can you get? *Learnin'ta read is a whole lot like goin' blindt, Trude.* I was the one needing help!

Never did I know what would spew forth from this unassuming man. I only knew it would be wisdom personified. His simplistic explanations were eloquent beyond belief.

He warmed my soul — and wearied my writing hand.

ROY CADDELL'S D-DAY

Roy Caddell knew he was but one of millions scattered across our country who can neither read nor write. He knew his chances for accomplishing his goal were slim at best when he walked into that library twenty-two days ago. He wanted more for himself. He would not settle for less.

We were there, Exam Day. Roy Caddell's D-Day. Once again, as I rounded the library corner, he was there. Pacing back and forth, back and forth. I had not seen him do that for weeks now, and my heart softened. I sounded my horn in familiar greeting as I whirled into the back lot. As he turned to face me, not a smile creased his face. He barely raised his arm in greeting. It was Day One all over again.

He approached my car as I pulled up, his white hat pushed far back on his head, not a twinkle in his eyes. As I rolled down my window, he began talking — fast.

"Boy. I shore don't like this none. I don't know if I'm readt-y f'r this here 'r not, Trude. This is a big day now."

"I know that, Mr. Caddell. And I also know you are going to do just fine. I have looked everything over thoroughly and there is not a question on that test you do not know. What is so funny though, is that there are no extra test questions to cover all the additional material you have learned these past nine weeks. It is, as you say, Sir, 'a bunch.'"

"Yeah. I was tellin' Hazel this mornin' when I was tryin'ta study f'r this here, we done been off in lots a them other places w'th all the things you brung me, that we been studyin' 'n I been learnin'. It has been a bunch now, Trude. I'm not jokin'." He was beginning to laugh now, and that was good.

For once, when we were safely ensconced in the conference room, we did not sit and casually visit. I opened my teacher's text and went right to the task at hand. My friend was much too edgy for anything else, his face was solemn.

"All right, Roy. There are six parts to this check-up. Each one is short. Each question contained within the separate parts is simple. Each one is worth one point." He raised his eyebrows quizzically.

"All this means is that there are more than one hundred points to be earned on the test. We are going to take it slowly by sections, exactly as the textbook authors have presented it. They did a fine job."

"I shore do hope so, 'cause I'd like'ta show 'em how much I've learnt. How much you've taught me — so they won't fire you, that wouldt be real bad f'r me. I'd hate'ta break me in another teacher. There cain't be too many like you out there." I began laughing.

"Sir. You know by now they will not fire me. But, you are right, I rather imagine there are no other tutors quite like me. They know what they are doing. I do not. They are qualified. I am what is called *a pure novice*. In fact, they should give you extra points for having worked with me. You have earned them." He missed my joke.

"That's what I meant, Trude. There aren't no more like you. I done got used'ta you, and I don't wanna start in on another one now. I just won't come back no more."

"That is not funny, Mr. Caddell. If anything were to happen to me, you must come back and finish what you have started. Delia would find you another teacher. She is so impressed by your efforts, as is everyone at this library. You have been committed and faithful."

"Well now, Trude. I don't know as I couldt do that. . . ." This, I was not expecting. I looked him squarely in the eye and quietly stated my singular case.

"Roy Caddell, this one thing I ask of you. It would kill my very soul if you were to let drop all that we have worked so hard to learn. Please, you must promise me this one thing. . . ." That was all I could get out.

There were tears in my eyes as I turned to face him. Then, as I spoke it, now as I write it. This alone was more important to me than almost anything I had undertaken in my life. *This one man had to learn to read and write!*

"Well, now. I din't know it would be so im-port'nt to you. I guess I can promise that. . . ."

"There are no guesses here, Roy. It is either Yes or No," I quietly said. My eyes never left his. He was silent a long moment, solemnly pondering what he never could have imagined. Finally, he answered softly.

"Then, it wouldt haf'ta be, yes." He warmly smiled.

"Thanks." That was all I could get out of my mouth. I do not think this man had ever considered how critical this was from my viewpoint. He knew now. There could be no misinterpretation.

"OK." I began, gathering my voice back to full strength for our task at hand. "They have divided this check-up beautifully into six parts: sounds, letters, words, listening, writing and reading." I shot my fingers into the air as I read off each category. He was counting. Sure enough, there were six.

"Now, on most tests, there is a score of one hundred percent. Here, the entire total number of points you can score is one hundred and fifty-eight. So, you can see that this is not a regular test at all. This is a guide, a gauge of sorts for what you have learned — much like an oil gauge or a tire gauge tells you something needs to be added, or subtracted. The same holds true here.

"From this evaluation, I will know what *I* need to do to further help you. And you will know what it is you need to work on. That, Sir, is all there is to it." He looked unhappily resigned to his fate.

"Are we at least agreed that this is not a bad thing? That perhaps, since there is no pass or fail, you can relax a tiny bit?" I hurled a warm grin his direction as he turned to display his first brightness of the day, a weak smile.

His test scores were nearly perfect:

Sound-Letter Relationships:	29 out of 29
Letter Recognition:	25 out of 25
Word Recognition:	25 out of 25
Listening and Writing:	27 out of 27
Writing Capital Letters:	24 out of 25
Reading Comprehension:	27 out of 27

Or, 157 points out of a possible 158! I shouted for joy! Roy was "over the moon." He slumped in his chair from relief and tension, as his grin encompassed the whole room.

"Boy! That warn't so bad. But I shore din't think I'dt do that good. What'do you know? I have learnt somethin' after all. I cain't wait to git home 'n tell 'em how *real-ly* smart I am, they won't hardt-ly believe it. Don't know as I do ne'ther."

As he tucked his test paper away for proud display later, he kept shaking his head in utter disbelief. Suddenly, he turned.

"Trude. I think maybe I knowt a bunch a this stuff when I come in here. But, I din't know how'ta put it together, or where 'ta start. So, I gave up a long time ago on ever even tryin'. You got me start'd again, and I shore do want'ta thank you f'r that — f'r bein' the one. 'Cause we *have* come a might-y long ways here. We have. . . ."

He was semi-shuddering at the thought of where he had been only two short months ago: Out in a pasture talking to cows, and angry because he could not read or write.

I merely nodded at his words and smiled, as I reveled in his unbridled ecstasy. Fortunately, he continued speaking. I could not.

"Now. I think the main thing here is, I gotta practice what you been workin'ta teach me. And I gotta slow down, that's the main-est thing.

"You know, a couple a times late-ly, I've us'dt one a them fancy words you taught me. Now I like that! But, I gotta be REAL careful when I do, so's don't nobody ask me where I learnt 'em. It shore do soundt funny comin' from me. But I like doin' it.

"Fact a the business is, I like all of this here. 'Speshully now that it's over. I shore din't like it none comin' here this mornin'!" he exclaimed, reaching for his black satchel and white hat as we prepared to leave.

"Test day was scairy 'ta me now. You was gonna findt out how much I din't know. The better I did , the more it wouldt look goodt f'r you."

Roy Caddell silently reminded me of the Tunisian Olympian who, upon entering the track and field arena in darkened night, dead last in his event, said: "My country did not send me 5,000 miles to *start* the race. My country sent me 5,000 miles to *finish* the race."

Who was I to say that the event in which the man sitting beside me had entered himself, was not every bit as critical as the Tunisian's Olympic competition? Under bitter, trying circumstances, both men had pressed forward as if this were to be their last race. For my friend, it was.

Roy Caddell knew he was but one of millions scattered across our country who can neither read nor write. He knew his chances for accomplishing his goal were, perhaps, slim at best when he walked into that library twenty-two days ago.

He wanted more for himself. He would not settle for less. He had bridged his terrifying chasm. He had climbed his mountain and survived. With dignity.

He had won the blue ribbon at the fair. He was *finally* the brightest and the best in the classroom. A+ material. He loved it. He reveled in it. He deserved each accolade mentally heaped upon himself.

It would be a short drive home for us this day. I would return to stripping furniture. Roy, to his cows.

"I DO NOT LIKE 'TA START SOMETHIN' IMPORT'NT 'N NOT FINISH IT. THIS ED-UCASHUN STUFF IS IM-PORT'NT. I'M RUNNIN' OUTTA TIME, JUST LIKE THAT TUNISIAN GUY. WE BOTH GOTTA TRY 'N DO OUR BEST, THIS MIGHT BE OUR ONLY SHOT. IT'S KINDA LIKE GOIN 'TA HEAVEN. I DON'T WANNA BE A BIG SHOT WHEN I GIT THERE, I JUST WANNA MAKE THE TRIP."

R E F L E C T I O N S   A N D
I M P O S S I B L E   D R E A M S

Roy Caddell was there, at that point when it is easier to go forward than to go back. After "testa" day, there would be no stopping him. We were now into the second week of July. Not one time had I asked his long-term goals. His original answer might have been "short term," and I did not want to hear those words.

I do not think this man remotely knew what he was getting into as he drove into town that first day for lessons. If so, he quickly would have turned his brown truck around and headed the twenty miles back home. He did not, for one reason:

"I ain't never knowt one person who couldt'nt readt 'n write that din't want to, Trude. Not one."

To have said he was dubious of me that fourth day of May, 1994, would have been an understatement. I was the suspect, he the skeptic. As rapport developed between us, I teasingly would tell him that if he had passed me on the street before classes, he never would have nodded his white hat in my general direction.

"T'warn't no question about that. I'da thought you was one a them fancy ladies 'n that we wouldtn't never had't nuthin' in common. So, why bother? But, I see now I was wrong. . . ."

From Day One, my primary concern with this man was basic commitment. Would he stay for the long haul? If so, we would succeed. If not, we would fly right into the ground. I had no illusions that becoming a literacy tutor was a short flight. No one teaches an adult to read overnight. It is an impossibility.

Somehow, in my own busy days, I knew I could squeeze out hours for someone less fortunate that I. Over these last years, there never has been a time I did not look forward to classes. There never has been a day I did not want to go. I never have missed the hours spent with Roy Caddell — but oh, how I would have missed not knowing him. That would have been a tragedy of unfathomable proportions.

To say I am the same person as when I began teaching Roy would be untrue. I am a better person, a more sensitive and compassionate person. Now, I cannot imagine life without him.

All the while this man was on a quest to learn of a world outside his own, I was in shock at the world he was exposing to me. Sitting beside him day after day, I had nowhere to run. I stayed, and silently faced the narrow sphere around me — and tried to show him ways in which our two dissimilar worlds could co-exist and not collide.

As I have told Roy repeatedly, the sole given education affords to all is a chance to be more than, to make of yourself that which before was only a dream. That is all this one man wanted, a chance to overcome his nemesis. He had earned his the hard way: One day at a time for 23,161 prolonged days, sixty-four years. That is a very long time.

Never once did I hear him complain about his lot in life, his not being able to read and write. I would not have been so silent. Now, neither would he. How he has cherished the opportunity handed me on a silver platter. I had assumed education was a given. He knew better.

For Roy Caddell had spent a lifetime searching for the one key that would unlock his pain. He knew the answer had to be education. He simply did not know where the schoolhouse for grownups was. Driving the highways of life, he never once had stopped looking.

Through varied conversations, he came to learn mere education does not guarantee receptivity and openness. Uneducated people have no corner on the judgmental market. Bigotry abounds at all levels and in every strata of society. I learned such prejudice firsthand from Roy, he told me so. He had lived that life and he did not like it.

Slowly, he came to glean every person's other choice is closed minds and closed lives. Educated or not, too easily we all can become Boxes with No Lids. Narrow thinking rapidly turns into handicaps of hatred.

Roy came to recognize such potential within himself, I did not point it out. He was the one continually asking poignant questions as he tried to ascertain his own culpability. I merely provided reflective thought processes, options, and answers when I could.

Most reluctantly, the man cracked the doors and windows of his truck, his house, his life — because he did not want to continue living a lie. He did not want to bear the brunt and shame of the lowest echelon of society who cannot read and write.

He wanted more for himself, and was willing to work for it. I but kept his plate full and his nose to the grindstone. He never once complained. I guess he knew it would have done him no good.

Were I to pick the one thing that thrills me most about the education of Roy Caddell, it would be his loss of mental rigidity: How the outer boundaries of his thinking have been shoved, prodded, probed, outward, upward — while his inner framework has been gutted and quietly rebuilt, like one of those motors he works on so adeptly.

Our definition is "pushing out the parameters of your mind." Now you should see him twist his mouth to say that. It is a vision.

Though he speaks in a dialect I had not known firsthand, I will tell you flat out that Roy Caddell is the most eloquent man I know. Family and friends look askance at that statement. Eyebrows go up. Further explanation is always required, but it is true.

The man is an enigma, the wind. His mind is like trying to catch the rainbow. Good luck.

The greatest esteem I hold for this man, who worked his entire life with his back and his hands, is respect. He came. He tried. He persevered, against terrific odds. He gave this Education Business his best efforts. There were no cheap shots.

Together we turned dreams into reality, one step at a time. We pushed the envelope every lesson, by his choice and mine. For him, retreat was unheard of, unconscionable. He started this learning process, he would finish it — regardless the consequences or costs.

His fear of giving up surpassed his terror of trying. The one name he would never countenance for himself was "failure." So he hung on, often by his very fingernails. His scratches still resound across the blackboard of my mind. It is a grating echo, unnerving.

Who is to say why we do one thing and not another? I do not know why he came when he did, why he trusted me. He never offered, I never asked. Perhaps our shared dialogue is a tiny miracle, perhaps not. But, at the very least, our story is a bridge of hope and a passport to understanding — an example of reaching out, and reaching in: Growth and change, and a willingness to risk.

There is no way we could have foreseen such happenstance. Such would have been beyond our wildest dreams. For me, it has been the ultimate privilege. A panorama of perfect Kodak moments.

AFTERWORD

The universal creed of America is to pull for the underdog. Their touching human stories tug at our heartstrings and we quickly enfold them. Then, too often, we forget them. We would do well not to neglect the Roy Caddells sweeping our vast land. They are out there, hidden.

From the cities to the wheat fields, from the hamlets to the prairies, through the valleys, across deserts and high mountains, from ocean to ocean — we need to come to grips with the fact that these unschooled peoples have the potential to become our richest heritage. Sometimes the glass is not half-empty, it is full. It is not illusion, it is fact.

Too frequently there is a point of no return in all our lives. The same holds true for nations. Sadly, ours has lost one too many generations to illiteracy. We can ill afford to lose another. That cycle is vicious, unforgiving. It will not go away, even though we leave on our invisible blinders of prosperity — safely shielding us from the reality right outside our own front doors, down our streets and across our cities and towns.

These haunted people are out there, waiting for you, and for me. They need those with educations to teach them to read. A college degree is not compulsory. The only prerequisites are a willing heart and a discerning eye — to see behind their facades, their Masks of Shame.

Become a literacy tutor. Fight the insidious killer that is silently destroying our people. Together, we can turn an American tragedy into an American triumph. Without doubt, this wretched condition within our land desperately needs permanent eradication.

Nothing would please my dear Friend more than to feel he has had a minute part in this quiet revolution of learning, and of love. It would be his most impossible dream come true. But, once again, Roy said it best:

"The thing about it is, Trude, I think it's too late f'r me. But I'm gonna do it anyway. I'd hate'ta getta heaven 'n there be some writin' up there I couldn't readt — 'n then *me* go in the wrong gate! I gotta get me some insurance on that, 'cause I knowt full-well there's gonna be someone up there sayin,' 'You're not enunciatin' properly!' I knowt that. I gotta try 'n be readty."

Trust me, Roy. You'll be ready.

ROY CADDELL'S BIG WORD LIST

Begun in early June, 1994

"In my old life — it woulda sound'dt like a much bigger wordt." (The words in quotes are definitions transcribed as Roy either wrote them or spoke them.)

Conversation – "talkin' w'th one 'nother"
Listen – "be quiet"
Comprehension – "understan'dtin' one 'nother"
Connotation – "replacement for somethin'"
Communication – "talkin' 'n hearin' you"
Abbreviation – "shorten' up"
Attuned – "understandt each 'ther"
Exhilarating – "anxious to get goin'"
Incoherent – "not understandt'in co-rectly"
Unorthodox – "stray from the rules"
Extraordinarily – "little above average"
Enrich – "learn more"
Vocabulary – "how many words you know"
Appalled – "outrageous 'n disgust'd"
Enunciate – "put the T 'n E 'n S's on the word; talk plainer"
Attributes – "what you got"
Repetition – "do it again"
Facetious – "quick with an answer"
Bodacious – "a little bad and good"
Miraculous – "good"
Awful – "aw, shucks"
Validation – "good solid evidence; I got hope"
Certificate – "someone's gotta do it"
Certification – "someone who's qualified't"
Enigma – "somethin' that's just there"
Possession – "belongs to somebody else"
Parameters – "nothing tangible"
Profound – "deep thought"
Redundant – "saying too much a the same thing"

Cynical – "distrusting; leery; skep-tical"

Empathy – "feeling the pain"

Sympathy – "feeling sore f'r them"

Covetousness/Avarice – "greedy"

Continue – "you're on the right roadt"

Continuity – "a pattern"

Digress – "gettin' off trail"

Reverberation – "like an echo"

Diction – "don't talk plain"

Transpose – "they was in the wrong place"

Tenacious – "stayin' power"

Contemplate – "missed't one back there"

Concentrate – "study"

Absolute – "f'r shore"

Absolutely – "no question about it"

Observant – "I notice these things"

Condensed – "pretty clos't to what it was"

Outline – "hittin' high points"

Summary – "bring out the highlights — maybe add a little bit"

Scan – "look'dt it over real quick-like"

Cull – "I'm just gonna cull 'em"

Adjective – "tells you more 'bout some'thin'"

Contraction – "shorten' up "

Connote – "replace "

Diction – "say it in plain talk; say it so's I can understandt you. Country folks don't talk this way, Trude."

Comma – "whoa — slow down." "The only good one I've nearly met"

Colon – "hold't on . . . there's more"

Period – "The End"

Semi-colon – "country boy shorthandt"

Quotation – "my excitin' marks"

Exclamation Point – "bat 'n ball; somethin' im-port'nt"

!/""/;/./:/,/? – "them's all Creepy Crawlers!"

Evoke – "to mention or bring up"

Conjure – "how you see it"

Assimilate – "und-rstoodt"

Comprehend – "to understand"

Pneumonia – "very sick word — lung; soundts like somethin' you'dt get in a coal mine; bad"

Illiterate – "Me" *(From Illiterate came ILLITERAPHOBIA, an entirely new word that Roy made up! "Scar'dt of bein' illiterate." This was early March of 1995. Personally, neologists should include it in future dictionaries. Phenomenal!)*

Caustic – "witty and sharp"

Eloquent – "better quality of talking"

Elegance – "big shot/fancy lady"

Articulate – "like E.F. Hutton, when he speaks, ever'body listens."

Crux – "critical point "

Transpose – "in the wrong place"

Dubious – "Doubtin' Thomas"

Devil's Advocate – "kinda like startin' a rumor"

Ascribe – "Did that come from DESCRIBE? I know now they gotta come from some other wordt. . ."

Thrift – "clos't with a dollar"

Frugal – "cheep"

Unanimous – "all together"

Amnesia – "I for-git"

Viable – "big enough to do the job"

Capable – "smart enough"

Ampersand – "oh . . . that little mark. I seen that a bunch." (Roy never forgot this word thereafter, either its meaning or pronunciation. I was awed.)

Roy Caddell began another sheet of Mega Words with Dichotomy on October 31, 1995: *Dichotomy* – "separation of ideas"

My immediate reaction was shock. "Good gosh. What was I ever doing giving you that word?"

His quick retort: "I foundt it somewheres. It was on some trail we was on. I think it was when we was tearin' them wordts up." Then he grinned and rapidly added, "'N I'll bet we look'dt it up, Trude. . ."

Absolutely amazing. Both the man and his mind.

ABOUT THE TEACHER

Trude Steele Norman continues to teach Roy Caddell to read, and will do so until he is proficient and comfortable with his reading level. She is recognized for her volunteer literacy efforts, and recently was appointed statewide representative tutor to the newly formed State of Oklahoma Adult Literacy Advisory Committee. She continues to serve on her local library board and to do decorating for others. Stripping and refinishing furniture always will be a focus in her life. Her foremost loves are her husband and children, family and friends. Trude has left strict orders with her family that the countless numbers of yellow legal tablets, on which she has recorded years and years worth of notes and quotes from Roy Caddell, be guarded like Fort Knox — there is much of this story that remains untold. Trude feels that teaching Roy Caddell always will be one of the highlights of her life.

ABOUT THE STUDENT

Roy Caddell still lives with his wife in a log house he built on their acreage outside of Haskell, Oklahoma. He keeps cow dogs and cattle, and is forever "tinkerin' wi'th somethin' that needs fixin' 'round the place. I don't never get through." Every spring he is busy cutting hay, fixing tractors and birthing new calves, two of which he named Trude and Judge Mike. While he is not yet at the level of literacy he wants to attain, he is thrilled with his progress and will continue to attend school "as long as it takes. Now I've found there ain't nuthin' I'm not inter-est'dt in learnin'." His elation at seeing Susan L. Smith's illustration for this book cover was conveyed to his wife, when he told her: "I wish you couldn't be here to see my heart thumpin' — why, I almost look hand-some! This cover was shore e'nuff draw't after my big attitude change, 'cause I'm smilin'. I never look'dt like that befor' comin' down here." He and Trude will remain lifelong friends, schooling or not.